Treaty Promises,
Indian Reality

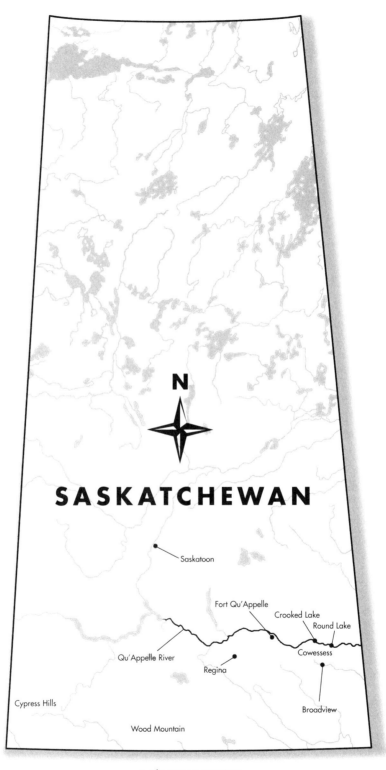

N

SASKATCHEWAN

Saskatoon

Fort Qu'Appelle

Crooked Lake

Round Lake

Qu'Appelle River

Cowessess

Regina

Broadview

Cypress Hills

Wood Mountain

Map locations are approximate.

Treaty Promises,

Indian Reality

Life on a Reserve

Told by Harold LeRat
Written by Linda Ungar

Purich Publishing
Saskatoon, Canada

Purich Publishing Ltd.
Box 23032, Market Mall Post Office
Saskatoon, SK Canada S7J 5H3
Phone: (306) 373–5311 Fax: (306) 373–5315
Email: purich@sasktel.net
Website: www.purichpublishing.com

Library and Archives Canada Cataloguing in Publication

LeRat, Harold, 1930–

    Treaty promises, Indian reality : life on a reserve / told by Harold LeRat ; written by Linda Ungar.

Includes index.

ISBN 1-895830-26-5

    1. Cowessess Reserve (Sask.)—History. 2. Ojibwa Indians—Qu'Appelle River Valley (Sask. and Man.)—History. 3. Cree Indians—Qu'Appelle River Valley (Sask. and Man.)—History. 4. Ojibwa Indians—Qu'Appelle River Valley (Sask. and Man.)—Government relations. 5. Cree Indians—Qu'Appelle River Valley (Sask. and Man.)—Government relations. I. Ungar, Linda, 1952– II. Title.

E99.C88L47 2005	971.24'4	C2005-904419-5

Cover design and map by Duncan Campbell, Regina, Saskatchewan.

Editing, design, layout, and index by Roberta Mitchell Coulter, Saskatoon, Saskatchewan.

Printed in Canada on acid-free paper by Gauvin Press.

The publisher acknowledges the financial assistance of the Government of Saskatchewan through the Cultural Industries Development Fund towards publication of this book.

URLs for websites contained in this book are accurate to the time of writing to the best of the authors' knowledge.

Second printing December 2005

Front cover photograph: see page 141. Back cover photographs: see pages 140 and 118. Chapter opening photograph: Distributing rations, 1910, Crooked Lake. In 1885, Yellow Calf from Sakimay took rations from the compound because the people of Crooked Lake Agency were starving. By the 1920s, only the old and infirm were provided with rations. The government considered the Indians had made sufficient progress in farming to sustain themselves. In the 1940s, welfare replaced the ration system. Saskatchewan Archives (RA253-6)

Contents

About the Storyteller

I am a treaty Indian from the Cowessess Reserve in Saskatchewan. I was born in 1930, the second youngest in a family of eight. My parents both died when I was really young, so I spent almost ten years at residential school at Crooked Lake.

When I was young, I wanted to be a professional jockey, but I grew too much, passing the 115-pound (52 kg) weight limit by the age of eighteen, so I did the next best thing: I started to train thoroughbreds for the racetrack. Eventually, I got to run my own horses on tracks across Canada, and my son Frankie turned out to be the jockey.

I always liked horses, just like my father. He was a horse trader. I started out by selling horses at the auction in Whitewood. Way back before we had horse trailers, I would head over to Whitewood and buy some horses at the auction, then break one during the twenty-five-mile (40 km) ride home to the reserve. I got a pretty good business going, breaking horses, just by word of mouth. I'd work a horse for one guy and he would tell someone else.

When you have thirteen children there are a lot of mouths to feed, so I did all kinds of jobs to make a living, from working for a transport company to running the community pasture to raising bucking horses for rodeo contractors. When I worked the big community pasture, there could be as many as a thousand head of cattle and horses in it, besides my own stock, plus I had a few smaller pastures going at the same time. At the peak of my ranching operation, I worked up to two thousand acres and ran over 150 head of cattle and 100 horses of my own.

The history of the Cowessess reserve has always been of interest to me. I learned a lot when I did research for the band on the spe-

The Storyteller Harold LeRat. Photo courtesy Harold LeRat

cific claims that resulted from the surrender of our lands in the early 1900s. That is when I started to think about writing this book.

I would like to help future generations understand the history of our reserve, have pride in their heritage, and know about Chief Little Child, who was the chief of our people at the time treaties were signed. A big part of the story I want to tell is how Little Child and my great-grandfather Pitawewekijik were together in the Cypress Hills but were forced to relocate to Crooked Lake in the Qu'Appelle Valley.

Most of the Indian side of our history was never written down, and the elders who could remember those times are gone. I am a rancher and a horseman, not a historian, so it was a challenge to put the pieces of the past together. I'm not a writer either, so I had to get help. If I made any mistakes in dates or names or situations, please accept my apologies. I hope my ancestors would approve of my efforts.

Harold LeRat

Acknowledgements

This book was Harold LeRat's idea and it is his story. I am the writer, the conduit, the one with the pen and the computer. Harold began to think about writing a book after he worked on the Specific Claim Process for his band, to research the surrender of Cowessess land in 1907. He wanted to capture the history of the Cowessess Reserve from an Indian perspective, to have more than just the colonialist interpretation of history available in archival records of Indian Affairs officials, and filtered from documents recorded by other non-Indians.

In the fall of 1995, Harold and Bert Sefton were visiting and talking about the book Harold wanted to write. Bert farms about 15 kilometres east of Marieval along the Qu'Appelle River, north of Broadview, Saskatchewan. His ancestors were among the first settlers in the Cotham area, a community on the north side of the valley south of Dubuc, and they had some of the first contact with the Indians of Crooked Lake. You will see recollections of those settlers in the pages to follow.

Bert mentioned my name and suggested that Harold get in touch with me to see if I would be interested in documenting his story. I used to farm in the Cotham area and knew several of Harold's relatives, but I had never met Harold himself. I lived in Regina at the time and worked in corporate communications, doing some freelance writing as a secondary business. Harold and I met on New Year's Eve, 1995, and have spent almost a decade working together on the manuscript. There were many hours spent in archives and museums from Calgary to Ottawa; hundreds of kilometres travelled to research the nomadic trails of the Cowessess Indians; trips to the Milk River in Montana, Fort Walsh, and the Cypress Hills and to Turtle Mountain in North Dakota.

I moved to Ontario in 2001 and then to Baffin Island in the Eastern Arctic in 2003. Distance created challenges to keep us motivated and in contact and to arrange to meet to review and rewrite the many drafts.

I would like to express my admiration for Harold and what he hoped to accomplish in writing this book. He kept me focussed on the final product and never lost faith in my ability to complete the task.

Harold and I would like to extend thanks to our families and friends who believed in this project and to Purich Publishing for bringing the final product to the public.

Thanks also go to the museum staff in Broadview and the Fort Walsh/Maple Creek area and to all the archivists, curators, and historians who assisted in locating documents and photos and shared their understanding of Saskatchewan history. Thank you also to the countless individuals who patiently answered our endless questions and brought history to life through their recollections.

Michael Keplin of Turtle Mountain is a descendant of Pitaweweki-jik and a relative of the storyteller. Michael has done a great deal of research on the American side of the LeRat family and generously shared his knowledge with us.

Calla Rowan assisted with elements of the initial research, and Marjorie Strandlund, Sharron Gerard, and Pat Guinn graciously proofread various chapters and drafts. Nicole Bussières and Louise Beaudoin helped with French-to-English translation. Maureen Lerat, Harold's daughter, read the final version, and her comments and suggestions were invaluable. Bert Sefton provided the history of the settlers in the Crooked Lake area.

Gordon Lerat, Jr., Harold's nephew, included me in the creation of Sacred Ground Tipi Camps, a cultural camp in the hills across the Qu'Appelle Valley from my cabin at Crooked Lake. I learned so much from that experience and used that understanding to assist Harold in writing this book.

Linda Ungar

Editorial Statement:

This book contains stories as told by Harold LeRat and recorded by the writer, including facts found in archival records and footnoted accordingly. Historical documentation recorded by government officials, priests, and settlers is incorporated with information collected by Harold LeRat during the course of a lifetime, gleaned by living and interpreted from the tales of others. The commentary is opinion-based and may differ from fact. We apologize for any inconsistencies.

The spelling of family and place names may vary from what is currently used, and there may be discrepancies in dates and circumstances of historical events based on conflicting, inaccurate, and illegible documentation, translation, oral history, and personal interpretation.

The language is conversational and reflective of what was acceptable in the past and in a less than politically correct environment. The author and storyteller recognize and appreciate the sensitivities of some readers.

There is no intent to malign or cast any individual in an unfavourable light.

Ancestors

My name is Harold LeRat. I am the son of Solomon LeRat, grandson of Zach LeRat, and great-grandson of Pitawewekijik.

Pitawewekijik's father was called Makadeshib (Black Duck). During the American Indian Wars, Makadeshib got killed. Pitawewekijik should have been hereditary chief of his Saulteaux and Cree band, but he was too young when Black Duck died. Even though he never became leader, people in the band referred to him as chief. They had respect for him.

My great-grandfather's people lived part of the year near what is now the Turtle Mountain Indian Reservation in North Dakota. They hunted and visited through Minnesota, moved on to Montana, and then went north to the Cypress Hills in the southwest corner of Saskatchewan. The annual journey continued from the Cypress Hills on to Wood Mountain; from Wood Mountain to Moose Mountain in southeastern Saskatchewan; from Moose Mountain back to Turtle Mountain.

Pitawewekijik's name is hard to translate. It is a sacred name that means something like "Sounding through the Sky" in the Cree language. In Chippewa, which is Saulteaux, the name is a little different, Pitowewekiizhik.

Pitawewekijik's people often spent the winter along the Missouri River. The missionaries had come west to spread the word of the Bible, and this particular spring, a priest was living with the band. As the story goes, they saw a group of Indians camped on the opposite bank. The priest wanted to know who was over there, and even though the river was wide and dangerous he asked if the Indians would build a raft so he could get across.

Pitawewekijik was a strong young man. He said that he could swim across the river and go to the camp. He was gone for more than a day, and they didn't know if he had made it or not, so his people were happy to see him coming back across the river. The missionary, who spoke French, said my great-grandfather was like a rat that would swim, a muskrat, and he called him "Le Rat."[1]

That is how we got the family name LeRat. After that, Pitawewekijik was called by his Christian name, Pierre (Peter) LeRat. The story was told to me by my Uncle Joseph LeRat, who heard it from his father, Zach LeRat, who was a child when his father, Pitawewekijik, swam the Missouri River.

LeRat Family Tree

Makadeshib

Pitawewekijik/Pierre LeRat (1820–1911)

m. Rosalie Contway (1835–?)	*m.* Emilie Siinpiins Desjarlais (1851–1944)
Francis (1865–?)	Ti-Pierre (1867–?)
Zacharie (1868–1930)	Ambroise ?
Joseph Lizette (1872–?)	Suzanne (1872–?)
Marie Helen (1875–?)	Emmanuel 1877–?
	Genevive 1879–?

Zacharie *m.* Marie Landry (1868–1948)

Solomon (1898–1936)	Veronique
Louis Roussin	Adele
Virginie	Joseph Norbert
Fideline Vitaline	

Solomon *m.* Mariah Peltier (1902–1935)

George	Frank
Florence	Elsie
Adeline	Harold
Clifford	Gordon
Mary	

1

"X" Changes Everything

Indians of many bands met up during the year to visit with extended family, to socialize, to arrange marriages, and to trade. In the 1870s, when treaties were signed, Pitawewekijik was in the Cypress Hills with many other Indians, including Chief Little Child, the leader that left us the legacy of the Cowessess Reserve. Pitawewekijik and Little Child may have been relatives, brother chiefs, but I don't know what the connection was between their families, only that they were both a mix of Cree and Saulteaux.

Each family had its own name and would say it in their own language, so Little Child was known by different names: Kawezauce (Little Boy) in Saulteaux, but Kawassis (Little Child) in Cree.

I don't know where Little Child came from, but I do know that he never got a Christian name from the priests, and the only reason they called him Cowessess was because it was too hard to pronounce Kawezauce.

The Indians were living their lives like they always had, travelling and hunting and stealing horses and fighting. It was the early 1870s and the Saulteaux and Cree were fighting in the Cypress Hills, the Black-foot and the Crow were stealing horses, and the North-West Mounted Police were moving in from the east to sort it all out.

The Canadian government wanted the Indians to give up roaming and hunting and agree to sign treaties. The white guys wanted our land, simple as that. They wanted the Indians on reserves and under control. They thought they could pay us some money up front and a bit on an annual basis and give us a few cows and some equipment and a promise to help us learn how to farm. They wanted us to stop hunting and live like the settlers on little pieces of land and grow crops. For that, we would give up our ways, our language, and our land. We were supposed to blend in and then disappear. They called it civilizing the savages, assimilation.

The chiefs didn't have much choice other than to sign the treaties. Métis and white hunters and traders slaughtered the buffalo just for the hides. The buffalo were disappearing, and the people were starving.

The idea was that once the Indians were all on their reserves, the land could be opened up to European settlers who would buy farms and start communities. The railroad could bring more settlers, and they would not have to worry about the Indians.

On September 15, 1874, many of the Cree and Saulteaux chiefs signed Treaty 4 at what is now Fort Qu'Appelle, Saskatchewan. Because they did not speak or write English, they were required to put an "X" beside their name to show their agreement with the treaty. This has always led to speculation about whether the chiefs actually did sign the agreement.

The land surrendered to the queen under the terms of Treaty 4 commenced

> at a point on the United States frontier due south of the north-western point of the Moose Mountains; thence due north to said point of said mountains; thence in a north-easterly course to a point two miles due west of Fort Ellice; thence in a line parallel with and two miles westward from the Assiniboine River to the mouth of the Shell River; thence parallel to the said river and two miles distant therefrom to its source; thence in a straight line to a point on the western shore of Lake Winnipegosis, due west from the most northern extremity of Waterhen Lake; thence east to the centre of Lake Winnipegosis; thence northwardly, through the middle of the said lake (including Birch Island), to the mouth of Red Deer River; thence westwardly and southwestwardly along and including the said Red Deer River and its lakes, Red Deer and Etoimaini, to the source of its western branch; thence in a straight line to the source of the northern branch of the Qu'Appelle; thence along and including said stream to the forks near Long Lake; thence along and including the valley of the west branch of the Qu'Appelle to the South Saskatchewan; thence along and including said river to the mouth of Maple Creek; thence southwardly along said creek to a point opposite the western extremity of the Cypress Hills; thence due south to the international boundary; thence east along the said boundary to the place of commencement.[1]

The treaty covered a big area of about 50,000 square miles (130,000 km²) in total. That seems like a lot of land, but it was a far cry from having the whole country to move around in, with no settlers, no railroad, no fences, no Canadian–American border, no restrictions, no government.

It took thirteen days for the queen's representatives and their military escort to travel the 350 miles (560 km) from Fort Garry (which is near Winnipeg) to Fort Qu'Appelle for the treaty signing.

Alexander Morris, Lieutenant Governor of Manitoba, David Laird, Minister of the Interior, and William J. Christie, Indian Commissioner, arrived on September 8, 1874.

Over fifty thousand dollars was paid out to about four thousand Indians to get them to settle on reserves. Each chief who signed the treaty got twenty-five dollars and a flag to show he was loyal to the queen. Each headman (a subchief, like a vice-president) received fifteen dollars, but only four men could collect this amount. Every other Indian man, woman, and child was paid five dollars. The deal was that every year in perpetuity (which means forever), each man, woman, and child would receive a five-dollar annuity payment.[2] We still get that today, once a year, a five-dollar treaty payment.

There were other perks too. If you were a chief or headman you were supposed to get a suit of clothing every third year. During the treaty signing, Commissioner Christie wrote, "The number of hats, and suits of clothing with flags for the various chiefs and coats for the headmen, according to the terms of the treaty, should be provided in time, as Indians remember all promises made to them and expect their fulfilments."[3]

Each reserve was promised ammunition and twine worth up to $750 every year depending on the size of the band. They would get agricultural implements, cattle, grain, potatoes for seed, and carpenter's tools based on the number of families who took up farming on the reserve.

The chiefs were supposed to select land for their reserve according to the number of people in their band and based on a formula where a family of five would be allotted one square mile (2.6 km^2) of land. Each reserve was promised a school as soon as the Indians settled on the land reserved for them. Liquor would be banned.

There were lots of promises.

Little Child arrived late for the gathering, with a group of around seventy followers. His band was made up of one chief, four headmen, and sixty-nine Indians when they came to the gathering to discuss Treaty 4.

Some of the Indians believed that the treaty was not final, that they were still negotiating and another signing would follow the next year. Little Child was one of the chiefs who did not want to sign yet or settle on a reserve. He knew that when the Ontario Indians signed the eastern treaties they got a twelve-dollar-per-person, one-time payment for using their waterways. Little Child wanted to hold out for a similar payment.

The Indians thought they should get a better deal, especially since the government paid so much money to the Hudson's Bay Company for what was called Rupert's Land. Back in 1670, a Royal Charter granted all the lands that drained into Hudson Bay to the Hudson's Bay Company. The Bay sold the land to Canada in 1869 for 300,000 pounds. The company kept the land around its trading posts and was able to claim one-twentieth of all fertile land. The Indians never could understand how the Bay owned the land in the first place, so how could they sell it? And why did the Bay get a better deal than the Indians?

Some copies of the treaty documents show an "X" beside Kaweza-uce.[4] This would mean that Little Child signed on September 15, 1874. Others just have the name and no "X," which would mean that they wanted him to sign but he didn't.[5] A lot of the old people are pretty sure he didn't sign in September 1874 in Fort Qu'Appelle. Maybe the officials thought he would sign later and marked his "X," or maybe he agreed later that year when he realized his people would not get annuities or rations if he didn't agree to the treaty. Even if Little Child didn't sign with the others, a pay list was issued for his band, with seventy-four on the list receiving annuities at Fort Qu'Appelle in 1874.[6]

At the time of treaty signing, Indians were assigned numbers called treaty numbers. Treaty numbers were used as identifiers, so it was important to get them right, but errors were common. Before Indians were given christian names by the missionaries, Indian names were difficult for government officials to spell, and some names sounded alike. Many times, an individual's treaty number was not the same from document to document and from year to year.

Here are some of the Indians in Little Child's band at the time of treaty.

#1   Cowessess (Little Child)
#2   Nepapheness
#4   Louis O'Soup

#5	Nequanequenape (First Quill)
#7	Kanaswaywetung (Two Voice)
#10	Equequanape
#11	Pitawewekijik (Pierre LeRat)
#13	Aisaican
#26	Zach LeRat
#31	Alex Gaddie

The government wanted Little Child to leave the Cypress Hills and take a reserve in the Qu'Appelle Valley to the east. There were seven families belonging to Wawasecapp's band already living near Round Lake and Crooked Lake on the Qu'Appelle River, and that was where Little Child was supposed to go. The Indians of Wawasecapp's band who lived in the area had made improvements to their land and didn't want to be moved from the valley. The government did not object to them staying put, but the plan was to move Little Child's band to the Crooked Lake area too.

Qu'Appelle is a French word that means "Who calls?" Before the French priests came along, the Cree called the Qu'Appelle *Kahtap-waosepe*, which means "What Is Calling River."

One of the versions of the legend of the Qu'Appelle, likely mis-interpreted from a story told by Indians, was that there was a spirit who travelled the river and that human voices could be heard crying out along the Qu'Appelle. According to the legend, an Indian brave was paddling along the river to his wedding when he heard someone calling to him. It sounded like the voice of his bride-to-be, and he answered, "Who calls?" The spirit called back with the same words, "Who calls?" The worry made him go faster to the village of his love. When he arrived, he learned that she had died but at the very end had called his name.

Another story was told by Loud Voice, one of the chiefs at Crooked Lake. According to Loud Voice, two groups of people arrived on op-posite sides of the Qu'Appelle and since they could not get across to visit, they shouted news across the water, and that is how the river got its name.[7]

The government didn't want the Saulteaux and Cree to get together in large groups anymore. It gave them too much opportunity to talk about the treaties and to complain about things when they gath-ered to collect their annuities. To avoid another gathering, the 1875 treaty payment was scheduled to be made at Fort Ellice (where the Qu'Appelle and Assiniboine Rivers meet near St. Lazare, Manitoba), Fort Pelly (south of the village of Pelly, Saskatchewan), Touchwood Hills (in the Punnichy, Saskatchewan area), Shoal River (in Pelican Rapids–Swan River, Manitoba area), and the Qu'Appelle lakes. All of those places were very far from Fort Walsh, where Little Child and his band lived.[8]

At that time in the Cypress Hills, the Indians were always sort of on the warpath, with different tribes fighting each other and stealing horses. It must have been interesting for Little Child to be chief, being a mixed-blood himself and with both Cree and Saulteaux in his band.

Christie didn't make it to Qu'Appelle until October 1875, and he came with a plan to get the Indians to settle onto their reserves. One thing he hadn't figured on was the number of Indians waiting there for their money, nearly five hundred lodges. The Indians wanted to collect their annuities, to talk about the terms of Treaty 4, and to get more information on what the treaties were all about. Because they hadn't planned for so many Indians, the officials had not brought enough cash to make the payments.

> We at once saw that the funds at our disposal would be inadequate to pay the annuities and gratuities and availed ourselves of the opportunity presented by the return of Major Irvine to Winnipeg to format a telegram on the 5th September requesting a further amount of six thousand dollars ($6,000) to be placed to our credit; and we may state here though out of the order of time, as we found after the first day's payments that we had still under estimated the number of Indians present, we transmitted, by special messenger on the 9th September for a further credit of fifteen thousand dollars ($15,000).
>
> To enable us to make the payments from day to day to the Indians we borrowed from Archibald McDonald, Esq., Factor of the Hudson's Bay Company, fifteen thousand dollars ($15,000) and afterwards finding this insufficient to meet the payments at the different posts a further sum of one thousand four hundred and ninety three dollars ($1493).[9]

Six chiefs who had not come to the 1874 signing were persuaded to sign an adhesion to the treaty (kind of an attachment) in 1875. Then they got their suits of clothing, flags, medals, and copies of the treaty, which they could not read anyway. They also were given ammunition, and provisions were distributed so each band could return to their hunting grounds.

There were five chiefs who showed "no desire to commence farming at present and gave no indication with regard to the localities where they desire their reserves to be set apart. They are plains hunters and depend entirely on the buffalo for subsistence." Little Child was one of those chiefs. He and the thirty-seven families in his band had no desire to leave the Cypress Hills.[10]

The next spring, the North-West Mounted Police stationed in the Cypress Hills received orders to notify the Indians that they could collect their 1876 payments on September 1 at Fort Walsh, about 300 miles (500 km) southwest of Qu'Appelle. Little Child was camped in the hills with his followers, over two hundred Cree and Saulteaux Indians.

In 1876, the Indians got together in the Cypress Hills to talk about the government's treaty obligations with Major James Morrow Walsh of the North-West Mounted Police. A member of Little Child's band, Louis O'Soup, acted as spokesman for all the bands.

I don't know where O'Soup came from for sure, but I've read that his father was the Saulteaux chief Keeseekoowenin, which means Sky Man or Sky Chief. Keeseekoowenin signed an adhesion to Treaty 4 and settled near Clear Lake, Manitoba. Wherever O'Soup came from, whether he was Indian or Métis, he must have had some schooling. He was a learned man and a very good speaker. He was much younger than Little Child, who was already an old man at the time of treaty, and they never really got along.

The chiefs from the Cree, Saulteaux, and Assiniboine bands in the southwest were all there together when O'Soup asked for a buggy and harness for each chief, cattle, and other farm implements, and farm instructors to teach them how to farm on their reserves and how to break up the land and plant crops.

O'Soup knew about trading with the United States, so he also asked to be allowed to bring goods from the American side without paying duties, and said that the half-breeds, the Métis, should be given the same payments and entered into treaty.

Once again Walsh told them that they would only get cattle after they lived up to the terms of the treaty and settled on their reserves.

The Indians also wanted to have their annuities increased; they knew the buffalo were thinning out. On April 20, 1876, Little Child, Little Black Bear, Blade Bone, Nesatunequawk, and Oushawapis sent a letter with O'Soup from the Cypress Hills to the Honourable Alexander Morris, Governor General of Manitoba. Someone must have written it for them. Here's what it said:

> We are now all gathered together in these Cypress Hills, the east-
> ward boundary of the buffalo and game country and we see with
> our own eyes that the buffalo are gradually dying and being killed
> off, and thereby our means of subsistence being reduced; hence we
> are moved to entreat the Queen our mother to have mercy upon
> her children, increase their annuities for it will be only a year or two
> before we can not make our living by that chase.[11]

The buffalo were not just disappearing. They were being slaughtered. When Indians hunted they used all of the buffalo. The hides
kept them warm and the meat filled their bellies. But traders and
hunters came in great numbers and killed the buffalo for their hides.
Robes and buffalo chaps were popular in Europe and in eastern Canada. The hunters could get good money for a buffalo hide. So they shot
thousands of buffalo, skinned them, and left the meat to rot.

It was a confusing time for the Indians. They wanted to stay in the
Cypress Hills, but there were rumours that treaty payments would no
longer be paid at Fort Walsh. They didn't know what to do. Travelling
the long distance to Qu'Appelle to pick up the treaty payments was a
big deal back then. Some of the Indians had horses, if their animals
hadn't been stolen. If they didn't have horses to make the trip to pick
up their annuities, it could be a long walk. Dogs were only good for
hauling the travois and for moving, so where the payments were
handed out made a difference. And it was a matter of principle. Little
Child wanted to be paid in the Cypress Hills. He considered that his
home territory.

The Cypress Hills are really close to the United States border, but
back then, the Indians didn't recognize the forty-ninth parallel. They
called it the Medicine Line and passed back and forth when they were
hunting and travelling. They didn't have to go through customs when
they crossed between the two countries like we do now.

When it was treaty payment time in 1876, some American Indians
collected at Fort Walsh, and the Canadian government got worried
they might try to do that again. The plan was to sort the American
Indians from the British Indians by some type of system of band
membership and to move the Canadian Indians north of the border
to eliminate the problem.

In 1876, the Dominion of Canada introduced an Act that still affects the lives of treaty Indians in Canada. Indians became wards of
the Crown and the Crown became the owner of reserve lands. The *In-*

Dog travois, Fort Walsh, around 1879. Stealing horses was common in the Cypress Hills. Indians used horses to carry loads, to travel, and to hunt. Dogs were also used to pull log travois carrying considerable loads when relocating the camp. Saskatchewan Archives (RA3951)

dian Act gave power to Indian agents to manage the reserves and more or less dictated every aspect of the Indians' lives. It took away their freedom to move around the country, to gather together and hold celebrations, to drink alcohol, and to sell produce as they saw fit. The *Indian Act* has been amended several times since it was introduced but it still affects many aspects of our lives as Indian people.

2

Leaving Those Hills Behind

Little Child was considered to be supportive of the government for the most part, and he expected the same in return. On May 25, 1877, Little Child arrived at Fort Walsh with concerns about the Assiniboines, who had about two hundred young men gathered in a war lodge with Chief Crow's Dance. For some reason, Crow's Dance and Little Child had had a disagreement and Crow's Dance refused to let Little Child move his fifteen lodges[1] away from the Assiniboine camp in the Cypress Hills. If Little Child left, the warriors said, they would kill his dogs and horses and cut up the lodges.

Little Child held a council with his headmen, and this is what he said at the fort:

> We made up our minds to move but are forbidden. When the children of the White Mother came to the country we thought they would protect us to move wherever we pleased, as long as we obeyed her law. The Governor told us when we made our Treaty with him. He also informed us that we had but one law to obey, and that was the law of the White Mother. Now what shall we do?[2]

Little Child and the council agreed they would move, and if there was trouble, they would see if the police would protect them. They took down their lodges, and as they were leaving, the warriors fired on the camp with guns and bows. They tipped travois and cut lodges, killed dogs, attacked the men, and scared off the women and children, who ran for safety.

Little Child warned Crow's Dance that he would report the attack to the police. Crow's Dance attacked him and said he didn't care about the police and he would attack the police too. Little Child went ahead and moved his camp north anyway and the Assiniboines headed east.

The morning after the attack, Superintendent Walsh saddled up and left to look for Crow's Dance and his headmen. By dark, they got to where the disturbance had happened, and by two o'clock the next morning, Walsh and his group came within sight of the Assiniboines' camp. Little Child had been sure Crow's Dance would resist, so Walsh was ready to fight.

According to written records, Walsh and his officers entered the camp early in the morning and took the Assiniboines by surprise, but the Indians had scouts out all the time, and I'll bet they knew exactly what Walsh was doing.

Walsh found Crow's Dance and nineteen warriors in the war lodge in the centre of the camp and arrested them; next, he found the others involved and arrested them; he then ordered breakfast and sent word to the chiefs of the camp that a council would be held at 6 a.m.

Long Lodge, Shell King, and Little Chief went to the meeting. At the meeting, Walsh questioned the leaders about why they had not stopped the warriors. The chiefs said they had tried to stop it but could not. At the conclusion of the meeting, Walsh told the chiefs that if in the future anyone wanted to move their camp, they were not to be stopped, and told them to warn the warriors that according to the law of the White Mother, anyone could leave camp when they chose. The government's people must have forgotten about these "orders" when a few years later they forced Indians to get a pass from the Indian Agent whenever we wanted to leave the reserve for any reason.

Walsh, his men, and the prisoners then went the fifty miles (80 km) back to the fort. Walsh noted in his report that every man of his detachment would have "boldly stood their ground if the Indians had made any resistance."[3]

Crow's Dance was sentenced to six months in jail. Some of the others got less time.[4]

Little Child had a hard time with O'Soup. O'Soup was at least ten years younger, and he was ambitious. He knew he could not be chief if he stayed in the Cypress Hills, and with the support of headmen Nepapheness (Night Bird), Nequanequenape (First Quill), and Kaykahchequn (Hides a Feather), O'Soup took part of the band and headed off to settle to the east at Crooked Lake.

When it came time for treaty payments in 1877, the band was clearly split: 307 members of Little Child's band were paid at Fort Walsh and 106 with O'Soup at Qu'Appelle. This left about thirty-seven families loyal to Little Child in the Cypress Hills. When the old chief went to collect his treaty payment, he talked to the government officials about O'Soup.

From what I've read and heard, most of the half-breeds and even the government's people considered Little Child to be one of the best Indians on the plains. He was old and respected. I've seen different opinions of O'Soup. Some considered him to be deceitful, someone who could not be trusted. That's how Little Child must have felt about him when he caused the split in the band and headed for Crooked Lake. But O'Soup was also a very good speaker and did a lot for the Indians to try to get a better deal.

That same year, the bands who settled along Crooked Lake were allotted reserves with about thirty miles (50 km) of frontage along the north side of the Qu'Appelle River.

The Qu'Appelle Valley is very bare on the north side and there was not enough timber or hay land, but trees grow tall and thick on the south slopes. The Indians needed wood for buildings and fencing, so the reserves were later moved to the south side. The bands in what was known as the Crooked Lake Agency would include Mosquito (which would become Sakimay), the breakaway group headed by O'Soup (to become Cowessess), Kahkewistahaw (which would keep the name of the original chief), Kakeesheway, and Chacachas (to become Ochapowace). Somehow the government reduced the length of the frontage allotted on the south side of the river to only twenty-one miles (34 km).[5]

Even after part of his band left with O'Soup, Little Child would not give up. He was determined that his remaining followers would collect their treaty payments for 1878 in the Cypress Hills and not at the Qu'Appelle like the government wanted. He was told his followers had to collect at the same location as the rest of their members, with O'Soup.

The Assiniboines who also camped near Fort Walsh, on the other hand, would still be paid at Fort Walsh because the government considered the Cypress Hills to be Assiniboine country at the time. Little Child was stubborn and would not give up his right to remain in the Cypress Hills. When he went to get the annuity payment, he and some of the Assiniboines asked to be given instruction on cultivating the land. Little Child was willing to try farming in the hills. The Indians knew the buffalo were disappearing and they needed to be able to feed their families.

By this time, the Indians were having a hard time surviving in the Cypress Hills, and they must have angered the new Indian Commissioner, Edgar Dewdney, with their constant reports about being hungry. The government wanted the Indians to realize that they were expected to work for a living. Dewdney's advice to them was to accept a reserve and settle on it and then a farm instructor would be appointed. I don't suppose that filled anybody's belly. You just can't change people from hunters into farmers overnight and expect them not to have good reasons to complain.

Little Child was still hoping he could stay in the Cypress Hills, even if things were tough. He wanted to start farming, if that was what he had to do, and he needed a reserve surveyed. Dewdney instructed a surveyor named Allan Patrick to map out both the Assiniboine reserve and one for Little Child in the Cypress Hills.

At first, Little Child chose some land about twenty miles (30 km) east of Fort Walsh, but that location had very little timber so he decided to try a location up Battle River, the creek Fort Walsh was built

Life was increasingly difficult in the Cypress Hills in 1878. The buffalo were disappearing, and the government pressured the Indians to leave the area for reserves to the north. Chief Little Child stubbornly refused to move his followers out of the area and offered to take a reserve near Maple Creek and start farming. Glenbow Archives (NA936-28)

25

on. James (John) Setter, a farm instructor, was sent to select the site for the buildings, but this site also proved unacceptable and Setter was told not to make any major improvements because different arrangements would likely be necessary. Nothing seemed to work for Little Child to select a reserve in the Cypress Hills, but he kept trying to find a suitable location.

This is how Walsh described the initial plans for Little Child's band in the spring of 1877:

> "Little Child," the Cree chief, who had intimated to me his intention in the spring of settling on a reservation, was also here [Fort Walsh], and had been waiting for some days to see me. In the spring he thought he would like his reservation about 20 miles east of Fort Walsh, but on visiting it and finding timber was very scarce, he thought he would prefer it up Battle River, the creek upon which Fort Walsh is built. I told him I saw no objection, and that, if the country was capable of raising crops, I would send an instructor there. He told me he was glad the Government had kept the promise made in the spring, that an instructor should be sent up, and he had remained in that part of the country purposely to see whether that would be the case. I was unable myself to visit the locality selected by him, but I sent Mr. Setter, the farming instructor I proposed to leave on "Little Child's" reservation, . . . to select the site for the buildings. On Mr. Setter's return, he did not appear to think favonrably [sic] of the location, so I instructed him to make but very slight improvements, as I expected different arrangements would be necessary in the spring.[6]

By November 2 when Walsh returned to the fort he said,

> I then inspected "Little Child's" reservation, to which I had appointed Mr. Setter, and found it was totally unfit for a farming agency or an Indian reservation. I determined then to send Mr. Setter to the valley near the police station which I had visited a few days previously, east of the Cypress Hills. I also sent word to "Little Child" and asked him to go and look at this location for himself, and inform Mr. Setter if he was satisfied with it.[7]

Indian reserves were basically run by the Indian agent, who was appointed by the government to manage the day-to-day business of the reserve and to keep the Indians in line. Some Indian agents were fair and decent, but others made life very difficult for the Indians. Early in the 1880s, the agents were given financial power to run the reserve and legal powers, like as justices of the peace, to hold trials and turn an Indian in to the police. They were in charge of the rations and who got them or didn't get any. It was the Indian agent that could keep an

Indian from getting ammunition for hunting or from going to visit a nearby reserve or selling a cow or buying a piece of farm equipment. It was all up to the Indian agent, from registering an Indian at birth to who got a house, to saying who was really an Indian and could or could not live on the reserve. They handled elections and surrenders and sometimes influenced the outcomes. Agents ran our lives and lived right on the reserves. In the early 1950s, the agent we had moved to Broadview so we had to go there to meet with him.

Farm instructors were also hired by the government to teach the Indians how to be farmers. I think it must have been hard for the instructors who wanted to help the Indians. The government directive was to turn us into farmers, but at the same time to be sure we didn't do too well and get to be competition for the settlers.

Five years after Treaty 4 was signed, there were nearly three thousand Indians from forty-two bands in the Cypress Hills. By now the government had hoped that all the Indians would be settled on their reserves away from the American border.

The policy was developed to get the Indians away from the Cypress Hills because the Canadian government was worried about the Indians causing trouble in the Fort Walsh area. Things got pretty uneasy, especially after the Battle of the Little Bighorn in 1876, when Custer went up against Sitting Bull and the Sioux. We know how that turned out for Custer, and in order to escape punishment in the United States, Sitting Bull hid out in Canada, in the Cypress Hills area.

The Sioux were camped north of the Canadian–American boundary, in the way of the northern movement of the buffalo, so the Canadian Indians were out of luck for meat or hides. They still depended on buffalo for food and clothing.

The American Indians claimed the buffalo were theirs, because the herds roamed south for the winter, but that was just migration. They thought the ducks and the geese were not ours either, that the birds belonged to the southern people.

Prairie fires could be very bad in those days. To keep the buffalo from coming north they made a big range fire. Fires started at different points, almost all at the same time. That scared the daylights out of the Indians because it just burned and burned and burned and burned.

After they got their treaty payments, large numbers of Canadian Indians headed south to meet up with any buffalo they might find.

There was no way the herds could get through to the Indians who had settled on reserves further north, so if they wanted to hunt, they had to go to the buffalo.

In addition to all the other problems, there were reports of scarlet fever along the trail. Those who had stayed at the fort, which included Little Child's band, needed help just to survive the winter. It is not like they could go anywhere to improve their lot in life. The Indians could not travel far without horses or supplies. They had to stay near Fort Walsh and beg for whatever limited rations might be handed out by the police. Not only were they hungry, but how do you feel proud when you can't even feed your children?

It was no better for the Indians who headed south in the fall looking for buffalo and spent the winter along the Milk River in Montana. They came back to the Cypress Hills starving and destitute. By spring 1880, as many as five thousand were around the fort.

The government tried to get all of the Indians to move out of the area, but those who came in from the plains were in no condition to go anywhere. The Indians who had been around the fort all winter were in better shape to travel than those who had arrived from the south, which was amazing considering the lack of rations. So, they were given supplies, supposedly to last the journey to their reserves, and sent on their way.

According to the reports, the Indians ate up the provisions, then went back to ask for more. Finally, by June, most had left their camps for their own reserves, accompanied by more rations and with police in charge.

Whether the surveyor was dragging things out at the request of the government or just behind schedule because of the bad winter is anybody's guess, but in the spring he began the survey of the Assiniboine reserve near Fort Walsh. When he was done and was on his way to Little Child's reserve to proceed with that survey, Patrick got a telegraph at the fort.

The department told him to go to the Qu'Appelle Valley instead and report to the Indian agent, Colonel Allan McDonald, to survey reserves, including O'Soup's. McDonald had appointed temporary farming instructors at Crooked Lake and File Hills. He was the first Indian agent to live with his family at the Crooked Lake Agency. McDonald had been a Hudson's Bay Company factor and he spoke Cree fluently.[8]

McDonald was supposed to be on his way to Fort Walsh. Patrick decided to wait there for him, so they would not miss each other along the trail. It took six days for McDonald to arrive, but Patrick did nothing on the survey of Little Child's reserve in the meantime.

Summer was passing, and by the first week in August, Patrick was on the way to Crooked Lake and File Hills, where the Indian bands were complaining that their reserves had not been laid out. McDonald wanted Patrick to get busy setting out those eastern reserves.

Patrick sent his assistant to Crooked Lake and headed off to do the survey at File Hills. The assistant must have planned for Little Child to join with O'Soup at Crooked Lake because, when the survey was completed on August 19, over sixty square miles (155 km²) were allotted. Treaty 4 set aside one square mile (2.6 km²) to each family of five; only ninety-six members were reported with O'Soup on the 1880 pay list, so he should have been entitled to less than twenty square miles (52 km²) of land.

Some of the people who had stayed in the hills with Little Child wanted to move to Qu'Appelle to join with O'Soup. Others wanted to stay in the Cypress Hills.

Little Child still didn't have a reserve mapped out in the Cypress Hills, but the Indians were put to work farming. The home farm began operating on sections 28 and 17 of township 10, range 26, west of the third meridian, about two miles (3 km) south of the town of Maple Creek. There were about forty cultivated acres; two log houses and a log stable were located across a wooden bridge that crossed Maple Creek from the cultivated area.[9]

Between Little Child's and Piapot's bands, there were over a thousand Indians for Mr. Setter, the farm instructor, to teach to farm. They started out growing a few acres of oats, wheat, barley, and potatoes, divided into twenty or so small gardens so that each Indian family could take care of their own piece of land.

The government farm supplies were not much good. The oxen were a total failure. They were so wild they couldn't be worked. There were no teams of horses that could be used for ploughing because every available animal was busy hauling provisions to camps of starving Indians.

In the summer of 1880, Mr. Setter managed to employ over forty Indians at the farm. The crops were excellent considering the seed was planted late and there was no rain for six weeks. The wrong barley seed had been sent, so the crop was touched by frost. Frost was a problem in the Cypress Hills.

Even the Indian agent had to admit that the Indians had put a lot of energy into growing a good crop. When he passed through Little Child's garden, members of the chief's family were tending cucumbers, corn, and other vegetables. Little Child's garden was written up in Indian Commissioner Dewdney's report.

Even though the Indians were doing pretty well at farming, Dewdney had not changed his mind. He wanted them all out of the Cypress Hills. In November 1880, he sent a letter to the superintendent general of Indian Affairs in Ottawa stating that the Assiniboines' crops were not satisfactory in the Fort Walsh area. He wrote that the grain—what there was of it—froze and was cut for hay. The potatoes yielded well but were all touched with frost and he didn't think they had ripened enough to keep over winter, so he told the Indians to use them for feed. Dewdney concluded that potatoes and barley could not be grown in the Cypress Hills area, and since so many Indians would need to rely on those particular crops, he thought it would be better to relocate the Indians to more suitable farming country.[10]

Whether or not the survey had been done for the reserve at Crooked Lake didn't matter to Little Child, and neither did Dewdney's assessment of the barley and potato crops the Indians had grown that year. Little Child still expected the government to survey a reserve for him where his band had started farming near Maple Creek.

The farm instructor, Setter, was given the word to encourage the Cree Indians to move north to where the rest of their bands had settled. Even though earlier the government seemed of the mind that the Assiniboines, lead by chief Nikaneet, were on home territory in the hills, the plan was that they should also be moved out. The Assiniboines did not leave, and as a result, Nikaneet is the only band still in the Cypress Hills today. If Little Child had refused to cooperate, like Nikaneet, then his band would have had to manage without any help from the government, no rations, no annuities.

Little Child tried to hold out, hoping for his reserve in Cypress Hills, but it was not in the cards.

By spring there were reports of large herds of buffalo heading north. It seemed to make sense to pay the Indians their annuities and let them hunt. That would take some pressure off the government and reduce the amount of rations they had to provide.

Little Child was not getting along with officials too well that spring. They said he was discouraging his men from working and that he complained about the rations and wanted a deed to his reserve. The old chief at one point threatened to give back the flag and medal he got when he signed treaty. On May 14, 1881, an Indian Affairs official complained:

> Little Child had been troublesome for some days previous to my going out, and had stopped his men from working, he complained of the quality of the flour and not being allowed a ration of tea and tobacco for his working Indians. He also asked me to give him a deed of the reserve saying he was alarmed that it would be taken from him and handed over to some other Indians. I informed him it was not in my power to accede to his demands and there was no cause for fear on that point so long as he worked the place properly, but that if he did not work it as it should be, I would hand it over to some person who would look after it properly. The next morning he again asked me for a deed of the place. I replied as on the night previous and he then went away apparently unsatisfied.
>
> When I had my horses harnessed and ready to start, he again called on me and stated he wanted to hand over his flag and medal, that he had made his living before we came in the country and could do so again. I told him he could give them to Mr. English and I would see about appointing a new chief, and one who would make his men work. I then drove off, thinking it better to let him return to his senses and see the error he had made. He is a proud man and one who would feel his position acutely.
>
> This morning his brother-in-law arrived from the farm, and informed me that Little Child was around the camp at daylight, warning his men to go to work. He also stated that some one must be influencing Little Child, as he had never seen him act thus before.[11]

In the spring of 1881, at Maple Creek, ninety acres were broken. The twenty-two acres planted to wheat grew to about four inches (10 cm) high by mid-May. They had sown some oats and a few thousand pounds (over 1,000 kg) of potatoes. The annual report of the Department of Indian Affairs stated that some of the Indians had ploughed and worked remarkably well, "which only proves that those who wish can learn as readily as the Whites."[12]

Little Child was worried. There were some of his members who wanted to join O'Soup at Crooked Lake and reunite the band. The department was still dragging its feet on surveying his reserve near the home farm.

The chiefs were told there would be no payments made in the Cypress Hills area that year and were asked where they would like to receive their payments. Little Child stood firm on being paid at Fort Walsh and also replied that he wanted a reserve and a schoolhouse in the Cypress Hills.

Farm instructor Setter was replaced by J. J. English, who encouraged Little Child with talk of building a school at Fort Walsh. He was given Little Child's assurance that he would round up his followers and that they would settle down and not go roaming all over the country. After the crops were in, the men of Little Child's band would help to build a schoolhouse. That school never happened.

Little Child had good reason for concern. The North-West Mounted Police were pressuring the government to relocate the reserves away from the American border. American and British Indians were mingling in what was left of the buffalo hunt. Indians on both sides of the border were starving as the buffalo became harder to find. American ranchers complained about the Indians from the Canadian side stealing livestock, and American Indians kept showing up for government assistance at Fort Walsh.

A large number of Northern Cree went south early in the summer expecting to get buffalo and to meet with those returning from the States. The Indians were seen as defiant and their complaints were considered to be unreasonable. Dewdney thought the half-breeds were influencing the Indians.

Then Chief Sitting Bull and his followers fled from the States into the Cypress Hills. Major Walsh, who was in charge at Fort Walsh, had to make sure Sitting Bull didn't cause any trouble, and even though Sitting Bull lived quietly in the area, the government still insisted the fort was too open to attack. Dewdney was told to close it down.

The government refused to give the Sioux any rations, and eventually the American Indians went back across the border. When word came that Sitting Bull and the bulk of his Indians had surrendered and been placed on American reservations, the Canadian Indians thought the buffalo would come north. They were anxious to be paid their treaty money at Fort Walsh in case the buffalo came in. Then they could buy ammunition and hunt.

This is how Dewdney explained it all in the 1881 Annual Report to the Department of Indian Affairs.

> I see no means by which we can prevent the Indians following buffalo if they come within easy reach as long as they have horses, guns and ammunition, neither do I think it would be advisable to force them to their reserves while there is a chance that they may make a living

by hunting, as we are not in a position to set them all to work and the result would be that we would be compelled to feed them and get nothing in return. In the meantime, land is being broken up on the reserves, and when the buffalo disappear, and they are compelled to settle down, we will be in a better position to receive them.[13]

According to officials, the Indians were basically satisfied with their treatment at the hands of the government. They made some requests, which the commissioner thought reasonable, for more tools and animals to work, but he was clear that only Indians who showed a willingness to work would have any of their requests considered.

Some of the chiefs who met with Dewdney in Fort Qu'Appelle were disappointed that they were not going to meet the queen herself, or the princess. The only people who dealt directly with the bands were the government representatives and the Mounties. The Indians wanted to meet this figurehead White Mother.

Even though some greeted Dewdney with gifts, they clearly stated that he should live up to the terms of the treaty, to take action on their concerns, to get them farm implements and the instruction promised. Dewdney would only consider smaller complaints; he didn't want to hear anything more of breaking treaty. He lectured on how the treaty was made for the good of the Indians and their children.

There was a lot of talk from various chiefs, and they weren't satisfied with the way things were going.

Standing Buffalo was an American Indian that came to Canada and stayed. He made this speech about how much he wanted to buy into the treaty promises:

> As you have come here, you will know that everything is good, and that we shall live now. I am on English soil and I want to ask for certain things in order that I may live by it. Please give me a church on my reserve for I want to live like the White people. And my children also a school where they can be taught. All the men of my band are very poor. My men are all naked and when winter comes they will be cold. We have not enough tools to begin to farm. For five years we have not had ammunition to kill game. Now that I am living on English soil, I try to live the same as a White man. I shake hands with them all strongly and I belong to the Great Mother. I came to this ground and was promised something to live on and have never received it.[14]

Loud Voice (Kakesheway) was frustrated and wanted the officials to pay attention to what he said:

I shake hands with the Almighty. I shake hands with the Queen. Let us live. I ask of you to let me live. As a Chief, I don't think I can do as I have a mind to. You will listen although you are only passing by. I wish you would put everything straight and right for us here. We are glad to meet together and talk.[15]

Pansung had already decided they were getting a bad deal and the treaty must be changed or they would not survive:

All these here say they can't live by the Treaty made by the first Governor. Those Chiefs told me in Council two days ago. We can't live by the First Treaty. I can't say that those sent here manage things badly, because you don't give them power to act as they wish. If you don't give them power, they can't help us. I am telling you our complaints. This is what they are afraid of, those chiefs. I see some things by which we can't live. The horses that had the scab have been given to the children to eat. That is why there is sickness and they are weak and die. Those chiefs here ask you to supply them with enough food. Those here wish that the Queen would open her storehouses to us.[16]

Day Bird stated:

Listen carefully. We wish you to grant what we ask for the women and children. Each man head of a family wishes a yoke of oxen and a cow. Needles and thread and useful articles for the women. Let us see the kindness of the Queen. There are many perishing with cold. We wish to be covered.[17]

The chiefs knew that they had to find a way to change faster so they kept begging for the government to give them the things they needed to become farmers. The Indians wanted to work. They knew the buffalo were not going to be there to feed them any more. It was hard to learn something new all the time, but the Indians were willing to try. They just needed the right tools so they could plant crops; if they had oxen they could pull a plough. If each family had a cow, then they would have milk and butter to eat. But the government didn't make it easy. They didn't provide what was promised or what the Indians needed to feed and clothe themselves.

Yellow Quill added:

I was glad to hear you were coming. I think my women and children will live now. Let us see the kindness you will show us here. I live by the ground here. Our forefathers could see buffalo and game all around. We used to live at that time. I am asking you and what is it that I ask. I do not understand the Treaty. Now I see what has been done to us. Our property has been taken from us. I can not live by what I was then told. You do not see horses because I have eaten them. We have also eaten our dogs. That is what your work has done for me. I shall not be able to live by the good words that are told me. You see one naked as I am. I have not got my coat. Perhaps he (the agent) wants to keep it. I cannot live on promises. Seven horned animals were promised me. I want all that I should have had. We only live by food. The only way we can live is by feeding us every day. They want the animals to live by and if they have food they need not kill them. We cannot live by the first Treaty; we shall die off. Provisions are the only thing that will make us live long.

Indians are taken from the reserves and if they commit crimes are put into prison. When starving an Indian took a piece of bacon and was punished. What is the reason you are in such a hurry?

Yellow Quill was afraid for the future of his people.

If we do not receive assistance this winter plenty of us will die. The first Treaty they say they cannot live by. I should like to know if the Treaty can be changed. I hope you will listen to what I am saying. I am afraid and certain that if you do not do what we ask we shall all be very badly off.

It is seven years since the Treaty was made. In the first, second and third years the gifts made are less and less. The first thing that ran short was food. The second ammunition also. Now we have no food and no ammunition and for that reason we cannot hold to the Treaty.[18]

Kanasis thought one of them should go to Ottawa to plead their case and suggested Louis O'Soup. He said Governor Morris had promised them help for twenty years and that they would never starve. He promised that if one of their people got killed there would be compensation and if there was property stolen it would be re-placed. Kanasis had lost ten horses and some of the people had been killed, but nothing was done. Kanasis said, "When a person breaks their promises that person is first to break the Treaty."[19]

Dewdney must not have paid any attention to those speeches because he reported that he found the Indians so contented that he was going to get one or two of them to go to Fort Walsh to tell the strag-glers left there how much the government was helping those Indians who showed that they could work.

Others offered to go, maybe even Chief Little Child, but Dewdney wanted to send O'Soup and said,

One man, a chief, stated that he was going at once to Fort Walsh and he would advise his young men to come home, and he begged some provisions for the trip. He started almost immediately, but I am sorry to say that on arriving at Fort Walsh, he acted in a manner diametrically opposite to that which he had voluntarily promised to observe, and it was reported to me that he had told the Indians that the Government was starving them and that some of his relatives had died last winter from the effects of starvation. I had not implicit faith in this man, and fearing he might turn traitor, I engaged the services of another chief called O'Soup, the leading man at the Crooked Lake reserve, and who hailed from the same locality as the first messenger. In O'Soup I had great confidence as he has been always found a most intelligent, hardworking and trustworthy man.[20]

About the same time, O'Soup made a request to visit Ottawa. Dewdney agreed with the agent, McDonald, that it might be a good idea for O'Soup and a few other chiefs to visit Ottawa, but it was just too expensive right then because they still needed to travel through the States. Maybe they would go later when the railway went through their own territory. By then, he suggested, there would be free passes for the Indians on both railways and steamers.

O'Soup didn't make that trip to Ottawa, but he was part of a delegation of chiefs who addressed the Marquis of Lorne, Governor General of Canada, during his visit to the North-West Territories in 1881. The governor general's wife was Princess Caroline Alberta, daughter of the White Mother, Queen Victoria. The story is that the province of Alberta was named after the princess.

The Indians always wanted to meet the queen who was supposed to love them so much and was going to take care of them. During the meeting, O'Soup talked about the lack of the rations, annuities, and government assistance.

A census of the Treaty 4 Indians done in 1881 noted O'Soup as having 34 people on the reserve at Crooked Lake and 331 absent, reportedly hunting at Fort Walsh. Little Child was recorded as a separate chief with 297 followers at Fort Walsh.[21]

When they first went to Crooked Lake, O'Soup's band survived by hauling supplies in the winter. In the 1881 annual report of the Department of Indian Affairs, it noted that O'Soup's band had 92 acres broken with 65 acres under cultivation. There were 127 acres already fenced and 40 tons of hay cut. They also had 17,000 rails cut, had one yoke of oxen, and nine huts. Those thirty-four Indians with O'Soup were really working hard at farming.[22]

By August, the survey of O'Soup's reserve at Crooked Lake was in the final stages.

In the Cypress Hills, the North-West Mounted Police were anxious to move the Indians away from the fort. They said the Indians wouldn't stay on their reserves but hung around the fort, waiting for government handouts and planing raids across the American border.

The railroad was coming, and with it an end to the Indians' roaming days. There were some Indians, like Chief Piapot, who tried to fight back by uprooting survey stakes; he even camped in the path of the railroad construction workers.

The Indians were destitute and had little fight left in them. The treaties made it almost impossible to hunt freely in the Cypress Hills. The buffalo were gone and farming was barely started. They were forced to comply with the government and move north to reserves in unfamiliar areas. A few wagonloads of provisions were enough to get most of the chiefs to lead their bands out of the Cypress Hills.

Over a thousand Assiniboines were relocated to the Battleford area to the north, accompanied by one constable and a number of supply wagons. Still, by late summer, many Indians had wandered back to the Cypress Hills. Almost three hundred teepees surrounded the fort during the winter of 1881. The government decided that the best course of action was to starve the Indians out of the area. Instead of seven days' rations for seven days, the Indians were given two days' rations every seven days.

According to the count of 1881, there were over 21,000 Indians in the North-West Territories. Half of them were on reserves and the others were reported absent. Of the missing Indians, it was estimated that about 4,000 were south of the line and would soon be driven back by the American soldiers, who were told to move the Canadian Indians out come spring. [23]

When the Indians received their annuities at the fort in the fall of 1881, they were told that Fort Walsh would be completely abandoned in the spring and that they had to go to their reserves in order to collect any future money. With no buffalo left to eat, the Indians were starving, sick, and gathered around the fort, completely dependent on the government.

The rationale for abandoning Fort Walsh was outlined in the report of the commissioner of the North-West Mounted Police in 1880.

> There is, to my mind, no possible doubt that the present headquarters, Fort Walsh, is altogether unsuitable, and I would respectfully urge upon the Government the necessity of abandoning this post with as little delay as possible.

In making this recommendation I am in great measure prompted by the knowledge of the fact that the Indian Department do not consider that the farming operations at Maple Creek have been successful in the past, and that they are still less likely to prove so in the future.

I am also of opinion, so I understand is the Indian Commissioner, that all the Indian Reservations (excepting those in the Macleod district) should be established further north. If then, Maple Creek Farm is to be abandoned and no other reservations located in the vicinity of Cypress Hills, I consider that retaining Fort Walsh as a Police Post, will act in a manner calculated to become detrimental to the policy of the Government, inasmuch as retaining this post offers an inducement to the Indians of the north to abandon their reservations and move towards Fort Walsh, knowing that a Police post is maintained and an Indian Agent stationed there.

Starving Indians coming in must, of course, receive aid from the Government. For this aid no return is given in the shape of labor, thus the Indian is in no way self-supporting, in other words, is fed at the expense of the country without his having to work, in fact encouraged in laziness. The Assiniboine and Cree Indians whom I may class as belonging to Cypress Hills, are all most anxious to settle on reservations, and naturally wish to remain about the vicinity of these hills. They are no judges of the fertility of the soil, and will remain as long as it continues to be a Police and Indian Department Post.

It has been proved beyond a doubt that the Cypress hills are not suited for agricultural purposes. The police force has been stationed here for six years, and yet there is not a bona fide settler within one hundred miles of Fort Walsh. In addition to the Police Force an Indian Department has been in existence for two and a half years, a large amount of money has been expended, in return for which there is little or nothing to show."[24]

The whole relocation out of the southwest had a lot to do with the whiskey traders. If they had left the Indians alone, it might have worked out better. The whiskey traders swapped horses for the Indians' buffalo hides, then gave whiskey to the Indians, got them drunk, and stole the horses back. When the Indians sobered up and found they were on foot, they stole horses from each other, from the American Indians, and sometimes from the whites.

Complaints were made to the American government in Washington that the British Indians were killing cattle, and there was some excitement among the cattlemen. I think it was likely that the horse-stealing raids might have killed a few cattle, but the losses probably had more to do with bad weather and the American Indians than with the Canadian tribes.

The whiskey traders were trying to get the Indians to come south. They promised reserves and buffalo to hunt. At the same time, the Unites States government instructed their military to drive British Indians back to the north.

The North-West Mounted Police made reports of horse stealing and warring between the tribes of American Indians and Alberta Indians and the Saulteaux and Crees and Assiniboines who were still in the Cypress Hills.

About eight hundred Indians, mainly the old and destitute, were getting a half-daily ration at the fort. Some of the hunters would pay occasional visits to get relief. Small game was plentiful in the fall of 1881 and there were some buffalo, reducing the pressure on the government to provide rations.[25]

However, the government was losing patience with the Indians in the area of Fort Walsh. According to the annual report from 1881: "They are the most worthless and troublesome Indians we have and are made up of Big Bear's old followers and Indians belonging to different bands in the north."[26]

> When they arrive they will be joined by all the other Indians in the southern part of the Fort, which will number over 7,000. They will leave their camp as soon as the grass is green and will rendezvous at some central point, I think Qu'Appelle. Runners will be in stating that numbers are starving on the road and ask that assistance be sent. They will arrive utterly destitute and we should have to do as has been done before, feed them. It is my impression that this is the last season they will go south and I feel that our ration list will next year be greatly increased.[27]

Big Bear was a powerful Cree leader who fought to try to get a better deal for the Indians. He was in the Treaty 6 area but refused for many years to adhere. Some of his band members were involved in the Frog Lake incident during the Riel Resistance in 1885, and even though he was not responsible for the deaths or involved in the attack on the settlement, Big Bear was jailed for treason. He died on the Poundmaker Reserve shortly after he was released from prison.

A doctor regularly visited the Maple Creek area to check on the health of the police stationed at the fort and on the Indian people in the hills. In the early 1880s, many children died of whooping cough. The Indians were scared by that and started to leave the Fort Walsh area.

There were stories of smallpox among the nomadic Indians, but that didn't turn out to be true.[28] Almost a hundred people were vaccinated:[29]

There seems reason to believe that we may be visited by this scourge. It has been prevalent in Minnesota and Dakota and has spread to Montana. I have accordingly, written for some fresh vaccine virus and on its arrival will vaccinate all the Indians in this district on whom the operation has not heretofore been performed.[30]

Other diseases were a problem too. When syphilis showed up among the police at Fort Walsh, they blamed the Indians.

A feature in the medical history of the past year, and one that is very much to be regretted is the introduction of syphilis among the men. This has already played great havoc, and still more serious consequences are to be feared if some means be not devised to prevent the spread of the disease. It was brought over from the other side of the line by the Cree and Assiniboine camps on their return here a year ago last fall. In the present state of the Indians, it is practically impossible to define the limits of the disease and effect a quarantine, but if new cases occur as frequently as they have been doing of late, some such decisive action must be taken. At the best, however, it is a subject surrounded with difficulties.[31]

The Indians had their own medicine. They knew the medicinal value of plants and had medicine men and healers. But the doctor thought he was winning them over. "The faith of the Indians in the White Man's medicine is becoming greater every year, as every year I am more and more often called on to attend to their ailments. Camps at a distance too, on the plains, often send to me for simple remedies, of which they know the nature and uses and the good effect of which they have before experienced." The doctor admitted the Indians had some amazing processes of their own, but were a bit skeptical of modern surgical procedures. "In surgery they are still tenacious of their own practices, and rightly so too, for many of them understand the subject pretty well" and would "not unfrequently obtain results which would be creditable" in western medicine."[32]

The British Indians (which meant Indians north of the border) had to give up their nomadic ways and settle on their reserves whether they wanted to or not. No more roaming back and forth across the Canadian–American border chasing the buffalo herds. No more freedom to go where they wanted. The Indian agent would soon decide if an Indian would be permitted to leave the reserve to hunt or to visit and whether an Indian could get a permit to sell wood or wheat or cattle. It would never be the same again.

A message was sent to Little Child at Fort Walsh to encourage him to move to the Qu'Appelle Valley. It was the Indian agent's job to get Little Child away from the Cypress Hills, and even though the old chief had few choices other than starvation, he didn't want to move to Crooked Lake if O'Soup was chief. O'Soup was a very, very good talker, but when the old chief, Little Child, spoke, the government people listened to him.

The plan started to unfold. Since the fort was to be abandoned, Agent McDonald took it upon himself to settle the differences between O'Soup and Chief Little Child. Here is what he wrote:

> For some time past I have feared difficulties through jealousies. When I was down there [at Crooked Lake] O'Soup was away at Ellice but I gave Mr. Setter instructions regarding O'Soup filling his land with strangers from other bands and spoke so strongly to Nepapeiness [Nepapheness] and Nequanequenape that brought the matter to a climax. Shortly after my return here, Mr. Setter came up with O'Soup, Nepapeiness and Nequanequenape and after a long interview a solution was come to. O'Soup tendered his resignation and promised to receive Little Child with friendship. Little Child was to be invited to come and occupy the reserve as chief with Nepapeiness and Nequanequenape as headmen. O'Soup intends starting a shop on the reserve and promised that he would always be willing to help his fellow Indians with his advice. I pointed to him that he might even in time, become enfranchised. There is every reason to believe that Little Child will accept the invitation and will be in with his followers this summer. Preparations are being made on the reserve for the arrival of those from the Plains.[33]

The government officials told O'Soup that Little Child would not live forever, so he should let Little Child bring the band back together and step down so that the old man could be chief at Crooked Lake. Little Child would be chief. Nequanequenape and Nepapheness could remain headmen. O'Soup was out. We know a bit about Nepapheness (Night Bird). He was an employee of the Hudson's Bay Company for years and was a respected buffalo hunter. Nepapheness lived from 1832 until 1920.

Near the end of May 1882, Little Child and eighty-five of his followers[34] set out for Qu'Appelle with the Assiniboine bands of Long Lodge and Jack. Jack was also known as The One That Fetched the Coat. The Assiniboines were headed for their reserves near Indian Head. The Indians were accompanied by farm instructor J. J. English and a small detachment of police. They travelled mainly with the help of the police horses and wagons, arrived at Qu'Appelle June 1, and were taken to their reserves.[35]

The Indian agent was permanently withdrawn from Fort Walsh in 1882, and the Indians were expected to collect their treaty payments at their respective reserves.[36]

For one last time, the government gave in to the plight of the starving Indians. After payments were made at Fort Qu'Appelle, Indian Agent McDonald left by train to distribute treaty payments at Fort Walsh. Little Child went along with McDonald to collect what was left of his band and get them to move to the Crooked Lake reserve. Little Child and McDonald arrived at Fort Walsh on November 1. It was getting late in the year to travel all that way back to Crooked Lake.

Little Child knew that even though some of the band members agreed to go to Crooked Lake in the spring, they might be persuaded, over the winter, to stay in the Cypress Hills, maybe by Chief Piapot and others who thought they could hold out for longer. Little Child was either tired of the fight or he knew there was no hope left except to side with the government and the Mounties. He tried to convince the commissioner to get the move to Qu'Appelle under way as soon as possible before freeze up and managed to round up 246 followers that fall.[37] Before arrangements could be made to transport Little Child's band to the end of the CPR line, west of Swift Current, the cold weather set in and work on the railroad stopped. The Indians had to stay in the Cypress Hills, and whether they starved or not didn't seem to matter.

Dewdney ordered the fort closed, eliminating the only source of provisions.

An exceptionally long and cold winter and the fact that some of the potato crop on the Qu'Appelle reserves froze meant that the Indians with O'Soup had it tough, even though they had gone to the reserve. The government had to come up with provisions for over two thousand Indians at the Crooked Lake Agency. It is said that the men who had to go out to hunt were pretty well clothed, but during the winter the women suffered without proper clothing.[38]

Plans were made in early spring to round up the rest of Little Child's followers and get them out of the Cypress Hills. Little Child had been right to try to get the Indians to move the previous fall when over 200 were ready to follow him to Crooked Lake. By May of 1883, he was only able to convince 112 members of his band to go with him via the Canadian Pacific Railway.[39]

As soon as the weather permitted, the Indians were to be taken to the end of the CPR track where rail cars would be provided to carry them to the railway station nearest to their reserve at Crooked Lake. That station could have been Wolseley, Grenfell, or Broadview, or even Whitewood. Instructions were prepared to "make the necessary arrangements as soon as the weather will permit, for the removal of Chief Little Child and his Band to the end of the track where cars will be provided for their carriage to the most convenient station to their reserve. Mr. Hayter Reed has been instructed to make arrangements with the C.P. Railway Company for the necessary number of cars."[40] They ordered dried meat sent to Maple Creek for distribution from there to points along the line.

It was hard enough to convince the Indians to leave the area and word of a railway accident didn't make them any happier about their trip out of the Cypress Hills. Not much is known about the accident, exactly when or where, and it is unclear whether any of Little Child's people were on the train when the accident occurred, but something happened while moving the bands to the Qu'Appelle area. The story I heard was that when the car tipped, a chief's wife broke her arm and others got so scared they would not get back on the train.

Here's what officials in Winnipeg wrote:

> I have the honour to inform you that great difficulty has been experienced in inducing the Walsh Indians to go to their various reserves, influence from many sources were strongly bearing upon those who were deciding to go north to change their minds, and not go. The railway accident which happened to those who were on their way to Qu'Appelle did a great deal towards upsetting their minds, and it was with great persuasion that they were induced to go farther, nothing would encourage them to take the cars again, so carts had to be engaged to do the carrying of those unable to walk.[41]

By the time the annual report was written for 1883, the Indians had supposedly adjusted to the change and were living in what the government called comfortable homes. Their hope was that the Indians would start to make a contribution and stop being a burden on the country. In that annual report it said, "Little Child went to his reserve with the intention of remaining permanently this spring and the short time he has been at work shows that he intends sticking to it, and he has already shown a good example to Indians who have lately gone on the reserve."[42]

It was hard to keep track of the Indians when they were moving around and out hunting at treaty payment time. That is partly why land claims have been made in recent years, to make up for incorrect counts of the number of Indians who belonged to a band. That made a big difference when the government was calculating the amount of land a reserve should have.

In 1882, 204 members of Little Child's band (including O'Soup's population) were paid at Crooked Lake; another 182 were paid at Fort Walsh, to total 386 band members. Once the band was completely re-located to Crooked Lake in 1883, the total population there was only 345,[43] so some of the Indians must not have moved to the eastern reserve. They were evidently not all planning to go with Chief Little Child come spring, despite the desperate conditions and the government insisting that they leave the Cypress Hills.

With all the people who showed up with Little Child, there were more now on the reserve than was planned for in the survey of O'Soup's reserve. They would need more land. The Indian agent, McDonald, took it upon himself to add more acres to the south end of the reserve, enlarging it from sixty-three square miles (163 km²) to seventy-eight square miles (202 km²) for the entitlement of 390 people. He officially reserved an additional eighteen sections[44] and recommended that the government compensate the settlers who were on the land.

Part of the problem was the Canadian Pacific Railway insisting that it owned some of the land intended for the reserve; as well, the agent evidently didn't have the authority to set aside land to extend the reserve. The whole thing dragged out for years, between negotiations with the CPR and with the settlers who were affected. Finally, on May 17, 1889, an order-in-council confirmed that it was Indian land.

> This reserve is situated south of the Qu'Appelle River, between the Canadian Pacific Railway and Crooked Lake. It is bounded by a line beginning at the south-east corner of section one, township seventeen, range six, west of the second initial meridian, and running north four hundred and eighty-two chains[45] more or less to a post and mound; thence east two hundred and ninety-eight chains and seventy links, more or less, to a post and mound; thence north four hundred and sixty chains, more or less, to the right bank of the Qu'Appelle River; thence north-westerly along the said bank of the river to Crooked Lake; and thence westerly along the southern shore of the said lake to a post thereon four hundred and ninety-eight chains and forty-three links, more or less, due west of the meridian of the last mentioned boundary running north; thence south six hundred and two chains and twelve links, more or less, to post and mound on the southern limit of the road allowance between township seventeen and eighteen, range six; thence west along said limit two hundred and eight-two chains and forty-seven

links, more or less, to the north-west corner of section thirty-one, township seventeen, range six; thence south four hundred and two chains, more or less, to the north-west corner of section six, in the said township; thence east two hundred and forty-one chains and ninety-four links, more or less, to the north-west corner of section three; thence south eighty chains, more or less, to the south-west corner of said section three; and thence east two hundred and forty-two chains, more or less, to the point of beginning, containing an area of seventy-eight square miles, more or less.

This reserve is well watered by Ecapo or Weed Creek, which flows through an immense wooded ravine and empties into the Qu'Appelle River. Along the creek, it is heavily wooded with poplar, balm of Gilead and some elm. The south-western part is undulating prairie with clumps of willow and poplar. The soil throughout is of choice quality. There are several mill sites on Weed Creek.

This reserve was originally allotted to the band of Chief "Osoup" and contained an area of sixty-three square miles, which was considered sufficient to meet the requirements of the band at that time. An extension of fifteen square miles was subsequently added by special order of the Department, as it was thought Cowessess would bring many Indians with him from the plains, when he assumed the chieftainship."[46]

There were four reserves all together in the Crooked Lake Agency; but only three chiefs: Little Child, Kahkesheway, and Kahkewistahaw. The other reserve objected to having a chief, so they did not have one, but the reserve was called Sakimay for the Indian who started it. Their chief spokesman was Yellow Calf. A few families in each band had settled on their reserves in September 1880 and so had already ploughed and seeded a total of 353 acres by the spring of 1883.[47] Setter was the farm instructor at the time. He must have moved over from the Cypress Hills. They say he was the son of an old Hudson's Bay man. He established the first agent's home farm at the Crooked Lake Agency.

Because of their experience farming at Maple Creek, those Indians that moved to Crooked Lake with Little Child were probably better farmers than the ones that took up residence earlier with O'Soup. That made for a good farming year the first year they were all together. Little Child's band sold 400 bushels of potatoes to a Broadview firm in August, at one dollar a bushel. The potatoes were shipped to Regina. Another Indian supplied 100 bushels of potatoes and turnips. Little Child's reserve purchased two mowers and two rakes. They cut their own hay and made enough to pay for the implements.[48]

The nearest mill to get wheat ground into flour was a long way off, about eighty miles (130 km), at Bird Tail Creek. Nepapheness sent ninety bushels there and O'Soup sent seventy bushels of the 1882 wheat crop to get it ground into flour. These two put in about thirty acres of crop each year and used their own seed. The two Indians, Nepapheness and O'Soup, declared themselves independent of further government aid. They were considered well off, and the government used them as an example, hoping other families would follow suit.[49]

The government was hoping Indians would get so independent they could become enfranchised. That way they would have to look after themselves and give up being Indians altogether. Some Indians wanted to live like the settlers and not be under all of the restrictions of the *Indian Act* and the control of the Indian agents. It even meant being able to vote, which Indians could not do until 1960. When you enfranchised, you lost your Indian status and were no longer able to collect treaty payments or live on the reserve. It was part of the plan to assimilate Indians, to make them just like the whites.

Even though those two Indians appeared to be successful farmers, Dewdney didn't think much of the potential for the adult Indian in general. He thought the only hope would be to work with the children. Residential schools were supposed to civilize the Indians:

> Experience has taught that little can be done which will have a permanent effect with the adult Indian, consequently, to create a lasting impression and elevate him above his brethren, we must take charge of the youth and keep him constantly within the circle of civilization. I am confident that the Industrial School now about to be established will be a principal feature in the civilization of the Indian mind. The utility of Industrial Schools has long been acknowledged by our neighbours across the line, who have had much to do with the Indians. In that country, as in this, it is found difficult to make day schools on reserves a success, because the influence of home associations is stronger than that of the school, and so long as such a state of things exists I fear that the inherited aversion to labour can never be successfully met. By the children being separated from their parents and properly and regularly instructed not only in the rudiments of the English language, but also in trades and agriculture, so that what is taught may not be readily forgotten, I can but assure myself that a great end will be attained for the permanent and lasting benefit of the Indian.[50]

There was already talk of a school to be situated in the Qu'Appelle district and supervised by the Roman Catholic Church.

All in all, 1883 was a year of change. The CPR reached the Maple Creek area despite the efforts of a few remaining Indians to stop the track. The capital city was moved from Battleford to Regina. The NWMP stationed at Fort Walsh were moved. Some went to Medicine Hat and others were assigned to Maple Creek in case there was trouble with the Indians. Buildings at Fort Walsh were burned, moved, or simply fell down.[51] Fort Walsh became more or less deserted.

In the fall, a telegram was sent from an officer stationed at Maple Creek to the commissioner of the North-West Mounted Police, stating that there were no Indians left at Maple Creek.

After moving the Indians out of the Cypress Hills, Dewdney observed:

> It is a matter of no wonder that such a strong stand should have been made against our repeated efforts to cause them to leave their old haunts, places associated with thoughts of freedom and plenty, whilst the buffalo roamed the Plains in countless numbers. Leaving those hills behind them dashed to the ground the last hope to which they had so strenuously and fondly clung, of once more being able to live by the chase.[52]

Indian Commissioner Dewdney had finally accomplished his goal, and he boasted in his writings:

> I look upon the removal of some 3,000 Indians from Cypress and scattering them through the country as a solution of one of our main difficulties, as it was found impossible at times to have such control as was desirable over such a large number of worthless and lazy Indians, the concourse of malcontents and reckless Indians from all the bands in the Territories. Indians already on their reserves will now be more settled, as no place of rendezvous will be found where food can be had without a return of work being exacted, a fact which tended materially to create much discontent among those who were willing to remain on their reserves, as well as to increase the laborious duty of our agents.[53]

3
Resistance

A surveyor by the name of Nelson arrived at Crooked Lake in early February 1884 with a work crew. They camped at Nepapheness's, where the farmer supplied the horses with hay and barley.

The plan was to redo the survey done previously by Patrick in order to give all bands frontage on the lake on the south side of the valley. They travelled the Qu'Appelle River along the northern boundary of Little Child's reserve and marked out a suitable fishing station. Five miles were cut from the lower part of O'Soup's reserve to give Kahkewistahaw reasonable river frontage and bottomland in the valley where the Indians had already started to farm.

It was a tough winter, particularly for the women, who did not have proper clothing. The surveyors sympathized when the saw the women fishing in the bitter cold. "While working at Crooked Lakes, the weather was very cold, yet many old squaws were seen at the fishing holes, endeavoring to catch fish. These wretched creatures seemed to be almost paralyzed with cold and were doubtless suffering from hunger otherwise they would hardly have attempted fishing in such intense cold."[1]

By fall, things were heating up. Louis O'Soup got word that Louis Riel wanted to see him and that there would be a meeting between the Métis and the Indians. O'Soup seemed willing to meet and responded on September 10, 1884, in French: "Cher Ami; J'ai entendu de dire qu'il voudrait me voir Louis Riel et auser qui font assemble les mitesses et les sauvages si j'ai de la faire qu'elque chose dit moi (toude cente) si il a besoin de voir Riel envoyer moi une ou plus vite que possible."[2] Translated, that would go something like, "Dear Friend: I have heard that he wishes to see me, Louis Riel, and also who is making the meeting with the Métis and the Indians. If I have to do anything tell me at once. If he has need of me, Riel, send me one as soon as possible. The note was signed Louis O. Soup, Crooked Lake, Broadview Reserve."[3]

Tension was building. Troops started rolling into the area. They were headed for Qu'Appelle, then north to deal with an uprising. The troops were after Louis Riel, of course. It was the time of the resistance of 1885.

In the early days of the uprising, a fellow by the name of Campbell came out west from Seaforth, Ontario, through Broadview, on a train with a boxcar loaded with cattle. Here is what he said about the trip.

> The next morning when we wakened we found ourselves in Winnipeg. It was a cold, bleak, frosty March morning, the 26th of March 1885. The first thing we were conscious of was the notes of a bugle about every few minutes. We wondered what the unusual sound was. One suggestion was that perhaps westerners were awakened in this way. We were not left long in suspense. The coach door opened and the C.P.R. policemen stood looking down the length of the coach and said, as though sizing us all up, "A carload of immigrants come to a land of rebellion." That remark brought most of us to life and I followed him out to the platform and asked him what he meant. He said there is some trouble out west in that Saskatchewan country with the half breeds and Indians and they have ordered the force here at Winnipeg to go out. They are leaving today. Then we knew that the bugle calls had been those of the 90th Regiment of Winnipeg.
>
> We were soon on our way west from Winnipeg and that night we reached Broadview. I spent the day in Broadview. I think there would be a dozen houses beside the station. It was a very long day for me. Sometime around noon a special train brought the troops into Broadview with General Middleton in command. They were bound for Troy (now Qu'Appelle). From there they would go north to the scene of trouble at Duck Lake, Clark's Crossing and Batoche. General Middleton wanted an Indian interpreter from the Crooked Lake Reserve to go along with him. The train was stopped at Broadview for an hour or so until the Indian could be obtained. The soldiers got out and took exercise. There were a great number of Indians and half breeds in the village that day to see the soldiers.[4]

Peter Houri, the farm instructor at Crooked Lake Agency, was assigned to Major Middleton's command as interpreter.[5]

The Indians were looking at trouble because the runners were coming from Battleford to get them involved in the resistance. O'Soup decided to go to Turtle Mountain. He wanted to be a runner (to take messages back and forth), but the agents would not let anyone leave their reserve, so he said he needed to go to Rolling River, near Roblin, Manitoba to hunt, and he was gone for months.

Riel's Ojibwa messenger Keniswayweetung arrived in Broadview on March 29, 1885, and teamed up with two local sympathizers to try to get the four reserves to help the Métis. Alex Gaddie and Nepapheness worked hard to convince the others that they should not go north to fight with Riel. Chief Kahkewistahaw also stood firm that his young men would not fight.[6]

Most Indians at the time could not read and write, but signs were posted notifying them not to get involved with the resistance.

> Whereas the troubles in the North have necessitated the bringing of large bodies of troops into the country to suppress the troubles, and punish those causing them, and when these troops meet any Indian off their Reserves they may be unable to tell whether they are hostile or friendly, and may attack them;
>
> And Whereas, runners are constantly being sent by Riel throughout the country spreading lies and false reports, trying to induce different bands of Indians to join him, by threats and otherwise;
>
> And Whereas, it is the intention of the troops to arrest and punish such runners wherever the same may be found, and it will be necessary for them, in order to accomplish this, to arrest all Indians, or any suspicious persons whom they may see, in order to ascertain whether or not they are runners from Riel;
>
> And Whereas, it is expedient that all good and loyal Indians should know how to act under the present circumstances so as to secure their own safety and the good will of the Government;
>
> Now, this is to give notice that all good and loyal Indians should remain quietly on their Reserves where they will be perfectly safe and receive the protection of the soldiers and that any Indian being off his Reserve without special permission in writing from some authorized person, is liable to be arrested on suspicion of being a rebel, and punished as such.
>
> ANY LOYAL INDIAN who gives such information as will lead to the arrest and conviction of any such runner from Riel, or any hostile bands of Indians, will receive a reward of Fifty Dollars ($50.00).

The notice was signed by E. Dewdney, Indian Commissioner; Regina, 6 May, 1885.[7]

The bands were uneasy and confused. At one time, as many as forty North-West Mounted Police camped in the area for over a week. The Indians were afraid they might be attacked. They must have heard stories of how the American Indians were attacked by soldiers and didn't want that to happen at Crooked Lake.

Men from Sakimay, Cowessess, Kahkewistahaw, and Ochapowace were reported to be holding war dances. Commissioner Dewdney investigated and found that the Indians appeared more concerned with putting in their crops than joining the resistance. That was a relief because the CPR mainline bordered the reserves for over twenty-five miles (40 km) and would have been an easy target for the Indians. Dewdney decided to supply seed for all the land the Indians could clear, to try to keep them busy and things running smoothly.

The settlers were also really worried. The Indians of the Crooked Lake reserves outnumbered the settlers in the area around Broadview and Grenfell. They knew that their lives would be in danger if the Indians sided with Riel.

Left to right, standing: Louis O'Soup, Peter Hourie; front row: Ahtahkakoop (Starblanket), Flying in a Circle, and Mistawasis (Big Child), October 16, 1886. In the early 1880s, O'Soup, an accomplished orator and spokesperson, led part of Chief Little Child's band out of the Cypress Hills to settle in the Qu'Appelle Valley. Later, Little Child brought the remainder of his band to reunite on what is now the Cowessess First Nation. Peter Houri was the farm instructor and a frequent interpreter on Crooked Lake Agency around 1884. Saskatchewan Archives (RB2837)

Some of the women and children went back east to wait out the trouble. The men armed themselves with rifles and rounds of ammunition and took training. They slept with their rifles in case of a surprise attack and even stacked a large pile of wood to light as a warning fire if anything happened, so people from the outlying areas could get together quickly.

Some of the men and boys from the area were hauling supplies from the railway at Qu'Appelle to northern army posts, and their women were left alone at home. Those who lived near the reserves were especially scared that the Indians would join the rebellion. They gathered at night at the Presbyterian Church at Grenfell and had a guard on watch outside. A train was stationed at Broadview, ready to rush to their aid if necessary.

> In 1885 many of the men and boys were away from home, trying to earn some extra cash on the transport, as it was called. They took their teams of oxen and ponies and hauled supplies from the railway at Troy to northern points where the army was stationed. Of course, there was bound to be some uncertainty as to whether or not the Indians in our districts would join the rebellion. The women who were left alone at home must have had a good deal of apprehension about the menacing situation. In homes nearer the Indian reserves perhaps there was more fear of the Indians. It had been verified that in 1885 the Indians raided the Mead's home for guns and ammunition. Mrs. Mead was alone at the time. On the same day the home of Luther Brown (one mile east of Mead's) was raided by Indians.
>
> Mrs. Robert McLean whose husband was away on the transport, had one of her young brothers staying with her for company. It was a month before her first child was expected. One Sunday morning, Mrs. McLean got up and to her dismay, she saw a tepee erected in her yard. What might the Indians do to her and her brother? Mrs. McLean did not venture out to milk the cow or to do the morning chores. They kept very quiet inside the house and around noon the Indians moved on, without molesting anything. This was in July 1885.[8]

Godfrey Rainville was the first settler to farm in the Cotham area, north of the Crooked Lake Agency. He arrived in 1884. In 1944, Rainville's daughter, Marie Adeline Jordens, wrote her memoirs about growing up near the reserves as new settlers continued to move in.

> Mr. Kendrick's sister had come out about the same time as we did (from England). I remember how she slept with me in a bunk under two upper ones, where the rest slept. Finding herself alone with her little nephew most all the time she had asked me to go over

at night, in case the Indians on O'Soup's reserve across the river should take advantage of her isolation. Having crossed the ocean all alone she shouldn't have been scared, but the rebellion had just been quelled and who knows how these people would react to new settlers. However, she was alone in the day time and we girls went to pick berries with never a thought of danger.[9]

Bertha Kendrick often heard the noise of the Indian tom-toms from the not-too-distant reserve and it must have had a frightening effect on her, this young English woman in the strange, lonely territory of Assiniboia. It is recognized by most of us that music or rhythms of another race are quite as enigmatic and incomprehensible and in certain surroundings as frightening as are foreign words and phrases. Bertha Kendrick, nevertheless, spoke highly of the Indians and their behaviour, in any dealings that she had with them during a long lifetime.

However, during these months there was a certain latent anxiety and tension prevalent among the settlers in most districts. Not only women but men too, became somewhat cautious about relationships with the Indians. Anything might happen.[10]

In the history of the Thomas Wilson family, early settlers in the area who lived on the Rainville farm in 1893, it mentions that when the Rainville's youngest child was born, the chief on Cowessess Reserve, Little Child, brought a small pony for him.[11] That baby was brother to Marie Jordens, author of the memoirs.

The settlers were lucky. The Indians didn't join the rebellion. Whether that had anything to do with the influence of the priests, the Indian agents, or treatment the Indians had experienced at the hands of the settlers is anyone's guess. It was likely more a credit to the chiefs.

In the Crooked Lakes Agency, Loud Voice's band had four men who went north during the resistance; Kahkewistahaw had five; Cowessess was considered loyal with one or two exceptions,[12] as was Yellow Calf from Sakimay, who decided to keep his followers neutral.[13]

Apparently, there was only one bullet fired near Broadview during the rebellion, and that was when an Indian shot through the store-house on Sakimay as a threat.[14] People were starving and could not get enough rations from the Indian agent. They knew he had all this salt pork, and with Yellow Calf as their leader, they took the rations out of the compound and gave them to their people. The Mounted Police were involved, and they were there the whole day at Sakimay, and on the second day, they told O'Soup to come and mediate between the Indians and the Indian Agent. That was the best oratory anybody had ever heard. O'Soup could talk his way into things he wanted or out of things if he had to.

Had the incident gone the other way and the Indians had risen up, it could have meant the end for the settlers around Crooked Lake and Broadview. Maybe more was going on that anyone knew. This account was written on behalf of Old Man Two Voice (Kanaswaywetung), in a record written in English called "Bringing Home the Bacon." It was found in the Oblate Archives, so it was likely documented by one of the priests in the late 1930s.

> I am going to tell how I have helped the Government. Once, over 53 years ago we had here a farmer instructor by the name of Mr. Keep and the old agency and ration house were over by where J. B. Sparvier's house is now. At that time, the Indians were hard up and weren't getting enough grub or rations so they got together and asked for an increase in their rations, but Mr. Keep refused. So they got together and planned a raid and went up to the Agency and asked again. They now threatened to help themselves to the ration house and when Mr. Keep refused, one man whose name was Ch-achekqwaquan picked up an axe and called the other Indians. He broke the ration house door and Mr. Keep who tried to stop him, grabbed him, but he wasn't strong enough as he was thrown down and choked while the other Indians ran in and took out flour, ba-con, tea, etc. and whatever they saw, they filled up their bob sleighs and drove away shouting and yelling.
>
> Then O'Soup and I went over to Mr. Keep and told him not to call the police, as he would make more trouble. Of course, he wouldn't listen and called the police. When the Indians heard of the police coming, they got together with their guns and ammuni-tion and then went down to the valley to one house and planned to wait for the police there. When the Mounties got down to the house, they weren't able to arrest the Indians. There were too many Indians. So, they returned for more police.
>
> At that time, there were two big Indian Commissioners, Mr. Tootney [Dewdney] and Mr. Reed residing at Regina and our In-dian Agent was Mr. MacDonald [McDonald] and he was quite old.
>
> Then, the Mounties came, over 20 of them, to arrest the Indi-ans. They came in bob sleighs. I happened to see them passing by. I jumped on my horse as I knew there would be trouble and raced to the scene.
>
> The Mounties, when they got down, found a line drawn on the snow, close to the house. This line, they were told not to pass. If they did, the Indians would shoot them.
>
> I just got down to the house in time. I heard the Indians shout-ing already, ready to fight, as the Mounties were almost on the line. I saw the Indians drawing the guns, ready to shoot. The Mounties

were ready too. I drew my horse just in between the two enemies and asked the Indians to 'wait awhile'. No one shot from either side. There is one Indian who saw me stop this fight and that is Peeni-pekeshig.

So, the Mounties gave up and went home without the Indians but the Chief of Police wired to the Commissioner and told him to come immediately or else they would spill blood if he didn't. So, Mr. Reed came down on the first train.

When Mr. Reed came he didn't have enough courage to go down to the Indians so he gave the Indian Agent the authority to go down and tell the Indians Mr. Reed wanted to see the Indians. The Indians agreed and came up (armed) to see Mr. Reed but he only wanted to talk to the two leaders who were Yellow Calf and Kanahwash. The other Indians waited outside ready to fight if their leaders were in trouble.

Mr. Reed asked them to go to Regina to see Mr. Tootney. I encouraged them to go and told them nothing would happen, so they went along with two other Indians Peenipekeshig and Gaddie. When they arrived in Regina, they weren't arrested and were treated nice and came home safe. When they came home, the farmer in-structor was fired.

The Indians during the unrest planned to kill off the Mounties that came to arrest them; then go to Broadview at night and mas-sacre the town. Broadview was a small town at that time and after they had cleaned up the town they planned to go along the railway and break it up so they couldn't get any more Mounties or help.

They didn't have the fighting apparatus like nowadays; they had a gun of iron or steel that would explode when it struck the ground. You could also see it flying. When it fell or exploded it threw out shots of metal flying all over.

They also had planned on asking the United States to help the Indians to fight the police. I can't tell the exact number of thou-sands of dollars I have helped save the Government during the olden days. I often think God is paying by allowing me to live to this age and see how things have progressed and I am sure it was him who gave me courage to help prevent blood flowing."[15]

At the time of the North-West Resistance, the government was very nervous about the Indians joining up with Riel. It decided to introduce a temporary ban on movement from reserve to reserve, to control things and to be sure they could keep track of Indians on their own reserves. If you wanted to leave, you had to get a pass from the agent and if you didn't have a good reason, in his mind, you didn't get to go. If you went anyway, it could mean the police would come after you. Even though it was supposed to be a precautionary measure dur-ing the uprising, it was not taken out of the *Indian Act* until 1951.

Some of the agents just looked the other way—they knew it was a ridiculous restriction—but others took it very seriously and the Indians on those reserves suffered. They could not go to traditional ceremonies or events on other reserves, or to visit relatives and friends. This law did a good job of wiping out the traditional ways.

There were ways around that pass rule. If you didn't get a pass, you could just jump a freight train and go. Besides, the agent didn't know where everyone was all the time. How would he know if you walked across to the next reserve?

The year after the uprising, Little Child died. Just before he died, the government gave him a new stove for his good behaviour and positive influence over the band.[16]

Little Child was probably about the same age as Pitawewekijik, my great-grandfather. We do not know for sure, but Little Child was already an old man at the time of treaty, over ten years earlier. He was known as a hunter, not a farmer. He tried farming in the Cypress Hills but never really took to it. The priests didn't make much progress with Little Child either. He did not accept Christianity and never followed the priests. They could not convert him so he was never given a Christian name.

Indians had just one name before the priests came. Those names sometimes sounded very much the same. For example, Pitawewekijik, who was my great-grandfather Pierre LeRat, had a brother with a similar sounding name, it just sounded a bit different. His name was Pieskanahapit, and he was given the name Francis. I think Francis died at Turtle Mountain, but the records say it was Pitawewekijik, which could have been my great-grandfather Pierre. It gets very confusing trying to figure out who was who back then. There are conflicting theories about Pitawewekijik and whether he was indeed the man who was known as Pierre LeRat or if he was instead Pierre's brother Pieskanahapit, who was called Francis. Francis was part of the band in 1879. It is possible that our family history search has confused the two men. For the purposes of this book, we have assumed that Pitawewekijik was the man who swam the river, got the name Pierre LeRat, became part of Little Child's band, lived part of his life in the United States, and was Harold LeRat's great-grandfather who died on the Cowessess Reserve in 1911.

In 1886, Little Child was paid annuities for one man, three women, two boys, and one girl. That means when he died he was responsible for three women, who could have been women other than wives, although he is thought to have had as many as five wives.

Louis O'Soup was recorded on the pay lists as having two wives in 1878 and from 1880 to 1883. One woman was absent in 1879, and one wife left him and the band in 1884.

Pitawewekijik first married around 1850 to Rosalie Contway, then took a second wife, Emilie Desjarlais.

Pay lists were the records used to keep track of how many people were in a family unit so the government could pay annuities. There were different categories. "W" stood for women, and there were columns for men, boys, girls, and others (which could have been in-laws or grandparents). On the pay lists, if the females listed under the W column were not wives, then they were other women the man was responsible for. The children were clearly identified as boys or girls, but the women were all lumped in under that W column with little explanation. The main wife was registered with the husband, but the second wife, the younger one, might be on her own with the children listed under her name but with no identification of the father. That makes it hard to trace family history and to do research for any of the claims processes.

When a man had two wives, the older one had more of a dominant role, but they had to get along. When the main wife got older, the man took a younger wife who could do more of the hard labour. The older wife cooked the meals, for example, while the younger one went to the bush to get wood and carried it home on her back. Maybe the thinking was that the first wife was the one who the man really loved so he took another wife so the favourite, older one didn't have to do so much work.

The priests put an end to that. At one time, a man could have as many wives as he could look after.

The wife of a chief was not allowed to look at another man. Women were sometimes put under what would be called house arrest today. They were punished if they were caught flirting. Most of the time the woman was blamed but occasionally a young man would get killed for paying attention to a woman. Women were not allowed to have another man unless he took them and looked after them.

Sometimes a man and woman would be in love with each other but the family had other ideas and would make them marry people they did not want to be with. If they disobeyed their families they risked being cursed, and that meant bad things could happen. In order to beat a bad curse, a more powerful person would have to remove the curse. But that was considered black magic by the priests, and they put an end to it when the Indians became Catholics.

It was common to be forced into a marriage. It was called giving away. But many of those unions didn't work out and the woman or man would eventually leave and live with someone else. They stopped giving women away around the 1920s, so the last ones that practice was forced on are either gone or are really old now. Indian Affairs and the church didn't agree with the giving away practice, making a deal for a woman. I suppose if the woman agreed to it and the man they got was not too bad, then it was a pretty good life and they stayed together.

Children were not named after their fathers with the same family name. They got their own names. Plus the women didn't have their husband's name like after formal marriages were done by the priests. That made it hard to do family lineage, especially when people lived together after the first marriage broke up because the kids often took the name of the man who lived with their mother. They were not his blood children; they were just raised with his name, adopted informally.

Before a woman got married she was listed under her father's treaty number and was identified as a girl. When she got married, she didn't get her own treaty number, she moved over into the W column under her husband's treaty number and in the comments section it said she came from her father's treaty number.

Sometimes on a pay list there would be a woman with a treaty number of her own. A woman was never named on the pay list unless she had never married and was over twenty-one. Then she could have her own treaty number and collect her own treaty payment. If she was a widow she got her husband's treaty number. Even if a woman went to live with a man, she went under his number.

When a boy turned twenty-one he got his own number and was identified as the son of number such and such.

People moved from reserve to reserve when they were allowed to and that was hard to trace. Sometimes when an Indian man got married, he would be accepted into the band where the woman was from and they would move there.

We could not find any evidence of where old chief Little Child was buried. One of the priests levelled all the gravestones at the Marieval Mission on Cowessess Reserve, then made a blueprint, which was

Indian graves located on a plateau on the Sheesheep reserve (Sakimay)
west of Melville Beach. The inscription on the grave is "Old Runnie 1929."
Broadview Historical and Museum Association (81:351)

lost so we don't know where people were buried. Little Child was
not Christian, and they refused to bury non-Catholics at Marieval, so
probably he was not buried in the graveyard.

Maybe Little Child was buried in the traditional way, sitting down
with his head sticking out, facing east so he could always be watching
the sun come up, with a little house built over his head.

Little Child was gone. It had only been a few years, and already the
Cowessess reserve, where the chief had been forced to move from his
preferred home in the Cypress Hills, was in danger of having land
taken away.

After the uneasy time during the resistance, the residents of Broadview figured the reserves were too close for comfort and they started
to ask Indian Affairs to relinquish all of township 17 and move the
Indians to the north. Indian Affairs knew it was not in the interests
of the Indian people to surrender any land and move them again, but
the political pressure was constant. This is where our illegal surrender
started taking shape.

The people around Broadview said that the district would receive a
new life if the Indians were removed. They considered the reserves an
obstacle to progress. As early as March 1886 the settlers were pressuring politicians to move the Indians back from the CPR line.

The deputy of the minister of the Interior wrote,

Settlers in the neighborhood of Moosomin brought to the Minister's attention the fact that the Indian Reserve in question lies immediately alongside of the Canadian Pacific Railway, that it would be desirable in the public interest and in the interest of the Indians themselves that they should be moved back six miles from the Railway; that this object can be accomplished by giving the Indians a greater frontage along the river, and that out of available land in that vicinity, which could be given them in a block, they could have this readjustment of their reserve made so as to give to each member of the band, an area not less than 160 acres.[17]

On a later petition it said that the reserves, being just one mile (1.5 km) from Broadview, seriously retarded the growth of that village; the reserves had much more land than they needed and no Indians lived on the land requested. The petition also stated that the Indians didn't use the land for hunting or agriculture. But that was not true. The Indians made hay and hunted and trapped in that area. All of the older Indians had claims to certain portions of that land. The people who wanted the reserve land pointed out that the sale of the land would greatly benefit the Indian people. The Department of the Interior seemed to agree with the settlers that it would be good for the Indians to be moved six miles (10 km) north. Indian Agent McDonald may have been anxious to satisfy the people of Broadview and the district, but he had served the Indians for some time and also realized he, as Indian agent, was responsible to see that the interests of the Indians were protected. He knew that if the settlers got their way, the Ochapowace and Kahkewistahaw bands would be giving up the

Alexander Gaddie.
Saskatchewan Archives (RB
586)

best of their hay lands, but it would be even worse for Little Child's Cowessess band.

He is noted as saying that if these lands were sold, no reasonable amount of money could compensate the Indians because their hay lands would be completely gone and there would be no way they could increase their livestock herds. At the time, the Indians were already quite successful in raising stock and had a number of animals. McDonald realized that the bands would have a large number of cattle in a few years and would need the hay lands.

In a later report, McDonald said that a number of Indians did live on the land in question. He maintained that the Indian people would have good grounds for being suspicious of a surrender, especially of Cowessess land. We had a lot of hay lands and the Indians knew better than to give that land up.

McDonald was also against giving up the land for settlement because he didn't think it was very suitable for farming. It just goes to show what he knew about farming because the land that Cowessess would eventually give up was some of the best land around. This all led up to the eventual surrender in 1907.

Since Little Child was dead, Louis O'Soup could now be chief, and he was elected by a majority of sixteen votes. Nepapheness was re-elected headman; Nequanequenape resigned and was replaced by Alexander Gaddie.

O'Soup is recorded as having said that

> he had always studied the best interests of the Indians. That he had always tried to set an example of work, and obedience, and begged them to do likewise, and not to listen to any bad talk about him, as such would always be uttered against a man in his position, but his actions would speak for him, and he referred to them.
>
> He referred to the money he had spent, individually, for the good of Indians, generally. That he was building up a home and provisions for old age, by hard work, and advised the Indians to do the same. To do the best to help themselves, not to listen to incendiary talk, but to the good advice he was giving them and also to that offered by the government, which has been and always will be, a good friend to them.[18]

Gaddie was a white man, or Métis, at least partly Scottish. He got hired as an interpreter in the 1870s and somehow ended up living on Little Child's reserve. The Indian agent gave him status in 1881, even though he was not an Indian. When he joined he had nine in his family, one man, one woman, four boys, and three girls.

Gaddie married Marie Rose Lavallee in 1884. He was a carpenter, a good farmer, and he must have been to school; some say he could read and write. Gaddie had a lot to do with the surrender of reserve land. He lived to be over eighty years old and died in 1917. His estate paid for his funeral and in the burial book he is listed as a farmer. Most others are listed as Indians, and Indian Affairs paid for their funerals.

Ottawa didn't agree with the vote to have O'Soup as chief and told the agent not to confirm the appointment until they were able to see how he handled himself. The agent was convinced that O'Soup had links to Louis Riel and that he had "encouraged the young bucks on his reserve to assemble and spend their time singing and dancing which was nearly always trouble,"[19] and to support the rebellion. Evidently, O'Soup was mentioned in some correspondence that had been found at Batoche which identified him as having sympathy for the rebels, so he was marked as a troublemaker.

O'Soup was a good farmer. He won first prize for cows and fat steers at the exhibition in Broadview. A couple of years later, his son, Peter O'Soup, took home the best ribbons at the fairs. They had the best horses in the country.

In the late 1880s there was a bizarre murder that led right to the Cowessess Reserve. James Gaddy, who was from Crooked Lake, and Moise Racette, who he had met in jail at Stony Mountain near Winnipeg, decided that while they were in Qu'Appelle they would get their photo taken. They could not afford it, though, because they had also bought a pistol.

Along the way to Racette's father's farm north of Wolseley, the pair stole two ponies and a mare from Hector McLeish. McLeish and Constable Mathewson of the North-West Mounted Police rode out to the Racette farm looking for the thieves. A few shots were fired, and McLeish was wounded. The two criminals hatched a plot to finish off the police officer, but that went badly when Gaddy missed his shot. Gaddy and Racette bolted. McLeish died, and a five hundred dollar reward was posted.

Armed posses looked for the two around Wolseley and into the valley. The Crooked Lake reserves seemed like a place they might go, but they had headed for Montana through the Cypress Hills. Once they made their escape, they took on other identities and lived on the run. The unpaid photographer who had taken their photo on the day

Settlers and Indians gather, possibly in Broadview, in the 1890s.
Saskatchewan Archives (RA18923)

they bought the pistol gave the photo to the police. It was circulated widely enough that they were caught.

They were sentenced to hang in the summer of 1888 and died on the gallows. The hangman was the same man who had hanged Louis Riel. Funny thing was, on the way to the scaffold they stopped to get their picture taken again.[20]

Marie Jordens's memoirs mention how affected the settlers were when the escaped criminals were on the loose.

> It was during that summer that the mounted police were hunting for two native lads who had stolen horses, then killed a mountie [sic] to avoid capture. These boys' parents lived on our reserve and it was thought that they might be hiding in one of the ravines close to the school. No one said much to me for fear I'd be scared, but I knew what was going on when a policeman would ride over and speak to Frank [Marie's husband, Frank Jordens] and once I opened the upstairs window to speak to a mountie at the front door, and he said, hello little boy. My hair being brushed back, I must have looked like one. Once on a Saturday morning I knew I was being followed by a mountie as I rode towards our homestead 6 miles away but he turned back when he saw me join the men at work. It took a long time for the mounties to find those boys, but they got them in the end. They always do.[21]

A press party was travelling around writing stories about the Indians in the fall of 1887. The reporter from the *Daily Sun* who recorded the events came from Sackville, New Brunswick. The other newspapermen came from various papers as far away as Quebec and the Maritimes and from as near as Regina. They attended exhibitions and headed out across the prairie looking for articles to write.

On October 1, the group met a Scottish Hudson's Bay Company officer at Crooked Lake who showed them his furs, supplies, and his own house. "He assured us that the Indians here are contented, and are rapidly improving their condition."[22]

Then they visited the home of an Indian farmer about two miles (3 km) from Broadview. I guess the people who signed those petitions saying the Indians didn't live close to the town and use the land were wrong after all. "Watchuk (muskrat) was the name of the owner. There was a fairly comfortable house built of poplar logs, the chinks plastered with a kind of red mortar. We found stacks of oats and peas and other grain and quite a number of cattle and horses. The farming however seemed to be done in a rather slovenly manner."[23]

They headed back to Broadview to the exhibition and reported that "Osoup, an Indian chief, got first prize for cows and fat steers. One of his steers was so fat as to seem almost deformed. These cattle were not housed in the winter but were fed outside."[24]

The press party went to several locations and had a lot to say about the geography, the weather, prairie fires, and the state of the Indians.

> The Indian problem does not seem to be a burning question here. We have been given every opportunity to see the original possessors of the country in several different lights. At the reserves over which Col. McDonald has charge we saw him as a farmer, with his house and stock. The impression left on our minds was that the Indian will yet make a farmer. At Indian Head we saw him in his paint and feathers and not particularly over clad, giving an exhibition of his musical and dancing powers, and of all the laughable, ridiculous and grotesque performances that the pressmen ever witnessed, this took the cake. In looking at this performance, the questions that would not "down" but kept to the front were: Are these folks human beings? Are they descendants of Adam? Are we brothers? Is it possible that men can descend so low?[25]
>
> It was at Indian Head that we saw the Indian Pow Wow dance, as they call it here: and he showed himself off in all his feathers and paint and beads and buttons and all sorts of finery. It was a mystery how he could put so much on him and keep it on when taking such violent exercise, and yet be half-naked at the same time.[26]

Everyone needed wood to cook and keep warm, and cutting wood helped band members make a living for their families. A man could cut wood all day, drag it out of the bush, haul it to a buyer miles away, and get $1.00 or $1.50 a cord, but he needed a permit from the agent to sell it. Broadview Historical and Museum Association (72:1789B)

Yet further along, at the Bell farm at Indian Head, the press noted that they saw another side of the Indian, "We found the noble red man pitching wheat to the thresher and performing the duty in much the same manner as his white brother. All were dressed as white men, except one old buck who handled the fork as if he didn't think much of civilization." The farmer told the press that the Indians were "good, at least fair workers, and that it would be almost impossible to run the farm without their help."[27]

This led the party to conclude that the government was doing a great job and there was hope for the Indians to become civilized.

> The feeling in reference to the Indian is very hopeful here. All or nearly all whom we have met think the problem is being gradually solved, and that the Indian will yet become a useful citizen. I have never heard the policy of the government questioned as it relates to the Indian here.[28]

"We were all surprised at the progress they had made as farmers and labourers," they wrote. "While all classes of the people seem ready to do them justice, the government appears to be doing their duty, in providing for their wants and their changed conditions.[29]

The press even wrote about gophers, described as

> a little animal something like our squirrel, but larger, called a go-
> pher. It cuts off the stock and sucks the sap or juices out of it and
> then leaves it. So troublesome have these little pests become in
> some localities that the municipalities offered a bounty of one or
> two cents for every gopher tail brought in. However, the tails come
> in so fast that one municipality was completely bankrupted. The
> funniest part of the affair was that the Indians, who used the gopher
> for food, objected to their wanton destruction, but they wanted the
> bounty, all the same. So they put upon the plan of catching the little
> cusses, cutting off their tails and letting them go again.[30]

The early settlers lived side by side with the Indians and often relied
on the generosity of people from the reserves. Marie Jordens remem-
bered the Nasayigans (Aisaican) as good neighbours to her and her
husband, Frank, when they were first married and living near the
reserves in the late 1880s. Mrs. Nasayigan was a midwife from the
Crooked Lake Agency who assisted when Marie's son was born.

> Mr. Bawden [a neighbour] had lent us a granary to live in. On the
> 29th of September, just as Mr. Bawden needed his granary to put in
> the grain, I had my first warning to decamp, and at once. It was 10
> p.m. and dark. We both took a load of bedclothes and walked the
> half mile home to mother. It had been arranged that I'd go over so
> she could look after me. Father (Godfrey Rainville) drove over to
> Crooked Lake for Mrs. Nasayigan, as mother was nervous. It didn't
> take very long with the horse and buckboard, for he had exchanged
> the old oxens and some cattle for a good team of mares. Well, when
> she arrived she had things fixed up to suit her. By four a.m. my little
> son was born.
>
> This being Sunday father went to mass after he'd taken the lady
> home on his way, then asked Father Lepage to come home with him
> so we could have the baby christened right away. They had dinner
> together and left at once. After driving a few miles, they smelled
> smoke. Was it a prairie fire? Sure enough and it was coming with
> the wind straight towards our farm. Well that was no joke. No fire
> guards around the hay or farm building. Racing the horse as fast as
> it could come, they joined Frank [Jordens] in trying to put out the
> fire here and there with wet sacks. The girls were letting the pigs out
> and corralling the cattle who were coming home on the run bellow-
> ing to beat the band.
>
> Our threshing had been done early that fall as we had the good
> fortune of getting a steam outfit from the O'Soup Reserve. Mr.
> Sutherland, the farm instructor was running it and had to cross
> the river at the west end of the lake, in the shallowest spot. [James

Sutherland was a blacksmith who was also resident farm instructor around 1886.] Well, about the fire. The fire had been put out by Frank alone for he had refused to give up, when suddenly the wind veered away from the straw, he gave it more pounding with the wet sack and the danger was over.[31]

The Indians were intrigued by the settlers, especially the women and children, because there were so few that came to the valley before the 1890s. The settlers, on the other hand, must have found it a bit unnerving by the accounts they wrote. Thomas and Elizabeth Wilson's daughter Mattie Sefton wrote:

> From Broadview we travelled the 16 miles through the Indian Reserve in a wagon, we forded the Qu'Appelle River which was the boundary of the Indian Reserve to the farm. The next day, the yard was full of Indians, who came to see the new settlers. I was terrified of them. They wanted to feel my long, fair hair. My little sister didn't mind them and let them lift her up into their carts and drive her around. My mother was afraid they would carry her off, but they were very gentle toward us and fed us maple sugar, on the tops of sharpened knives, from birch bark containers.
>
> We moved to a farm two miles east in the valley (the Rainville farm). The gophers were bad there, eating great patches in the crop so Dad got poison for them, and soon numbers were lying there dead. The passing Indians began to pick them up and made camp, skinned them and put them in a black pot hung over the fire. Mother was afraid the Indians would be poisoned too, and took the poison out to show them. They only laughed at her. The Indians passed along the valley in great numbers, some walking, some in Red River carts and buck boards, some riding on a sling contraption made by tying a rope around the pony's belly, to which two long poles were attached with a blanket put in a hammock-fashion close to the ends. Their supplies and the aged Indians rode there. We could hear the Indians approaching long before they arrived by the squeak of their Red River carts.[32]

Elizabeth Wilson's great-grandson, Bert Sefton, told me a story about when his great-grandparents first moved to the valley and lived in a one-room shack. She was cooking one day when seven or eight Indians just walked right in—didn't knock. When the young guys went hunting, they always stayed in a group. The Indians didn't have houses back then, just tents, and they were used to people all of a sudden showing up. The Indians were polite enough, they just sat around cross-legged against the walls and watched her cook and bake bread. She gave them something to eat and they got up and went out. They didn't say a word, but then, they couldn't talk English.

It wasn't acceptable back then for Catholics and Protestants or English and French to get together in a romantic way, so you wouldn't have found an Indian boy courting a settler's daughter. That would mean trouble. It was interesting to read the Rainville history to see the young people were still thinking about the possibility even if that was all it was. Marie Jordens pointed out a flirtatious incident in her memoirs and it made me laugh because I knew the later generations of the families involved.

The story happened before there was even a school for the settlers' children up at Cotham (the district on the north side of the valley, directly across from Kahkewistahaw). Three girls, I think one was Marie's sister and the other two were the Bawden girls, got quite a surprise from a couple of Indian boys who had been at the Bawden farm for lunch. "The girls had admired their get up, hair nicely braided with rings, weasel tails interwoven, etc. gave them a frivolous look and the girls started making remarks about how fine they were and how they wouldn't mind having one of them for a beau, never thinking for a minute that the boys understood English."

Later in the day when the girls were out walking,

> they heard the galloping horses and Indian yells right behind them. As they got nearer, the girls saw them waving their lariats above the ponies['] heads, then swinging them in their direction, circling around to prevent them from going on and stopping right in front of them. They started to talk English, saying "come on girls get on my pony, I'll be your man." When the girls tried to break through they'd round them up again. Still they were nearing the edge of the bluffs, so as soon as they were in sight of the house, they rode away towards the valley. Which all goes to show that these boys could take a joke! But the girls had really been very much frightened, and it had given them a lesson too.[33]

4

Warrior Farmers

The Indians were getting the hang of farming by around 1890. That year the crop was the best yet. All of the reserves together on the Crooked Lake Agency threshed almost 6,000 bushels of wheat. They had over 600 bushels of oats, around 300 of rye, 98 of peas, and 30 of barley. There were also 2,461 bushels of potatoes, 1,325 of turnips, 186 of carrots, and 483 of garden produce. During the winter, the Indians sold more than 4,000 bushels of wheat for over $2,000 and bought supplies, mainly flour.[1]

O'Soup retired at the end of his three-year term in 1891 after losing to Kanaswaywetung. Joseph LeRat and Ambrose Delorme became headmen. The Indian agent was not happy about the election results and made that clear to the band. He thought they should have re-elected O'Soup as chief and Gaddie and Nepapheness as headmen, because they had done a good job before. O'Soup was back in the good graces of the government. The concerns about his loyalty during the resistance were forgotten.

The agent was worried about their choice of Kanaswaywetung as chief since he was one of the only ones left on the reserve who still hunted instead of settling down to farming. "He was an Indian who had never shown a desire to farm, and was the only one of the band who preferred making a living from the hunt instead of by farming, which in the present state of the country and of the Indian race, gave a most pernicious example."[2]

There did not seem to be any way around the election outcome as long as things had been done properly or until the new chief showed himself to be unfit. It was Indian Agent Reed's opinion that the trickery of white elections was gradually moving into Indian elections as well. He said that the Indians were unsettled, that the best men were not always chosen, and that they were kept from standing up for what they believed to be best in order to be popular. Reed was inclined to want to do away with elections altogether. The Indian commissioner agreed that an election of a chief and headmen was not compulsory. It was not that the government was looking to go back to a system of hereditary chiefs, but they would like to have seen the position of chief abolished altogether.

In October 1891, O'Soup was elected again, but only as headman. Out of twenty votes, O'Soup got thirteen. He was way out in front of Baptiste Henri with four, Nepapheness with two, and Gaddie with only one vote. O'Soup declined the headmanship.[3]

Births on the Crooked Lake Agency exceeded deaths that year by thirty-two to twenty-six.[4] The Indians seemed to be healthy, at least healthier than the year before. There were 608 Indians on all the reserves of Crooked Lake Agency, and together their annuity payments came to just over $3,500.[5]

The Crooked Lake Agency sold 260 bushels of potatoes and planted 800 bushels in the spring of 1891.[6] The Indians ate the rest, along with the garden produce, including carrots, and turnips, and they fed the remainder of the root crops to their livestock. They had about 160 acres in summer fallow and just over 100 new acres broken. Some of them used their farm earnings to improve their houses, buying lumber for flooring, windows, stoves, chairs, etc.

There was not much hay to sell, as the weather was not good. The agency stock totalled 103 oxen, 109 cows, 2 bulls, and 210 young cattle under government control, and privately owned stock totalling 7 oxen, 59 cows, 3 bulls, and 83 young cattle. The Indians also owned four Canadian horses, two geldings, and two brood mares, all on the Cowessess reserve. Throughout the agency, there were 171 Native ponies, some improved by crossing with Canadian horses. The cattle herd was getting a better bloodline too with the help of the agency pedigree bull supplied by the department.[7]

Cowessess earned $1,426.33. That was the most of the four bands. Ochapowace made $834.35, Kahkewistahaw $1,275.19, and Sakimay $1,088.57, to total $4,624.44, a collective increase of $1,812.18 over the previous year.[8] There wasn't much income from trapping furs as some of the old trappers had to stay at home and look after their stock now that they were farmers.

It was a really early spring in 1891. Seeding began on April 7, a week earlier than the year before, and all spring work was completed by May 20. Cowessess had 251 acres in crop, Kahkewistahaw 120, Ochapowace 145, and Sakimay 122. They had almost 500 acres of wheat, as well as peas, potatoes, and turnips, about 20 acres of rye, some corn, barley, chicory, and of course the gardens.[9]

After spring work was done, the Indians got busy repairing old fences and building new ones. When fencing was finished, everyone who could spare the time went out to collect seneca root, also called snakeroot. They made six hundred dollars and had a good time getting away from the farm work to where they could make camp like years ago.[10]

A gristmill had been built at the agency with a steam engine for power. The Indians paid for their milling with wheat bran or cordwood for currency.

It didn't take long before the Indians decided they wanted to get rid of their new chief, Kanaswaywetung. Some of them got together and wrote a letter to ask what to do when they weren't satisfied with their chief. Kanaswaywetung had only won the election by one vote, and now they wanted him to resign. Some of his voters had been under the impression they were supposed to be paid for voting for Kanaswaywetung and when that didn't happen, they changed their minds about him being chief.

One Indian said he had voted for the chief and then was cheated out of ten dollars. Another said the same man who encouraged him to vote for Kanaswaywetung picked a fight with him after the election, in Broadview, and others noted that the ringleader in charge of getting Kanaswaywetung elected had been seen gambling. There were also references to some of the Indians supporting the rebellion and stealing horses, and rumours that the chief had been known for stealing livestock.

A band member said that the chief had asked him to steal horses across the line and sell them to American Indians and that the chief had told him that he would rise in rebellion if he could. Yet another said one of the headmen chased a big drove of cattle into his haystacks and they ate ten tons of hay. The upshot was that band members felt the chief was not honest.

Kanaswaywetung was also in trouble because he would not pay Gilbert Gaddie for a dog Gaddie had returned to him. The chief had said he would take the dog back and return the ten dollars Gaddie had paid him if the dog he had sold him was not up to warranty. According to Gaddie, the dog was no good but he did not get his money back.[11]

Everyone was complaining about everyone else. The Indians were asked if they would let the commissioner decide what to do about Kanaswaywetung. Three of the headmen agreed but one thought that there should be no chiefs or headmen at all and then the Indians could be equal. The chief finally agreed that the commissioner should settle it even if he decided to abolish chiefs and councillors.

O'Soup spoke on behalf of band members who had signed that letter making charges against Chief Kanaswaywetung and some of the headmen. He supported getting rid of the positions of chief and headmen and said that the money spent on the positions should go to the whole band.

The commissioner disagreed with giving the band the money. The Indian commissioner decided that even though there might be reason to remove the chief and councilors, he wasn't prepared to do so at that time.

Cowessess Reserve had 142 residents in 1893. The same number were born and died, which was 6.[12]

About this time, that big disagreement heated up again between the CPR and the reserve, and we lost the land near Oakshella, where the tracks crossed the reserve through the southwest corner of section 3, township 17, range 6, west of the second meridian. About thirty acres south of the track were cut off from the reserve. The CPR argued that they should be issued the patent because the railroad was there before the reserve was surveyed.[13] Indian Affairs could not verify that the reserve was surveyed prior to the railroad. In the end, we give up about fifteen acres and got paid $38.33,[14] about $2.50 an acre.

The department started to really push the Indians to take location tickets. If an Indian got a location ticket it meant he could occupy and use a piece of reserve land. The Indian still didn't own it. Reserve land is Crown land. The agent had tried before to explain the advantages, but the Indians were concerned that taking a location ticket might mean that their personal property could be seized—it was exempt from seizure on reserve land under the *Indian Act*. "The agent took advantage of such a representative gathering of the Band to open up the question of taking up location tickets for their separate farms on the reserve, and fully explained the advantages of doing so, which he had informally done many times before. The Indians wished to be informed whether Section 22, Chapter 28, means that all personal property is exempt from seizure and if assured by the Indian Commissioner that their present position respecting seizure for debt is impaired. The Agent promised to ascertain this fact."[15]

It was another election year and the department continued to try to get rid of the offices of chief and headmen. The band was just as determined to keep the positions. Hayter Reed, the commissioner, was still trying to get his way and complained that Agent McDonald was not doing everything he could to discourage the Indians from electing a chief and headmen.

McDonald didn't see that it was his fault. He thought the Crooked Lake Indians knew what was best for them and were advanced in their political thinking. "Indians of Cowessess possess some members a good deal in advance of other Indians in perspicacity. They know I have no say as to whether they shall have chiefs and headmen or not."[16]

The Indians believed the right to elect a chief and headmen was part of treaty. Some of the government officials thought they should try to bribe the Indians, give them tea and tobacco equal to the amount paid to the chief and headmen. Maybe they could find a loophole to eliminate headmen, based on too small a population. The Indians did not go for that plan, but the agent was supposed to keep trying to persuade them.

O'Soup had been either chief, headman, or band member for nearly twenty years. He could not see any real advantage to the present system, and he continued to make his opinion known. He thought the band should get rid of the chief and headmen and adopt a proper band council. Trouble was, very few band members agreed with him.[17]

On November 5, 1894, Nepapheness was elected chief, with sixteen votes; Alex Gaddie and Ambrose Delorme were elected headmen. O'Soup's bid for the position of headman got him only one vote.[18]

That was a dry year. Ochapowace harvested 205 bushels from 102 acres; Kahkewistahaw got 270 bushels from 113 acres; Cowessess did a bit better with approximately 1,300 bushels from 255 acres; and Sakimay brought in 188 bushels from 70 acres.[19] Of the almost 2,000 bushels harvested, 100 were oats and only about 15 barley. They sold about 450 bushels of the wheat to buy food and clothing.[20]

The gristmill ran for a couple of weeks in early December then closed down until warmer weather in March.

Hay crops did poorly, but enough feed was put up to winter all the reserve stock that was left; about 90 head of Cowessess cattle had been killed by a prairie fire in July. A lot of their hay land was also burned. The agent sent the Indians up to the Leech Lake Reserve to make hay. That was about 40 miles (65 km) to the north. They managed to make over 200 tons to help get through the winter.[21]

Even with the drought, the Indians who took their cereal and root crops to the agricultural shows in Whitewood, Broadview, Grenfell, and Regina did very well competing with the settlers. Everyone was suffering from the lack of rain, both settlers and reserves.

O'Soup was sick. He and Alex Gaddie went to Regina so O'Soup could ask Commissioner Forget for a pass to leave the reserve. He said he wanted to go hunting. When the Commissioner asked where he wanted to go, O'Soup told him he wanted to go to Pine Creek, near Swan River, Manitoba and that he didn't know how long he would be gone, it would depend on his health.

At that time, O'Soup did not plan to transfer to the Pine Creek band, he only wanted a pass. O'Soup's son Peter was left in charge of the farm at Crooked Lake. It was one of the better farms on the agency, with a good spring, cows, chickens, pigs, and a barn with eleven stanchions.

That year, 1895, there were 158 residents on the Cowessess reserve. Six were born and four died.[22]

The band had three treaty cows and four oxen. Cows and oxen were moved from one farmer to another after they had a couple of calves. That way there was equal opportunity to build up individual herds.

For example, a treaty cow was moved from Equequanape to Norbert Delorme on the understanding that it would be taken away if it was neglected and not kept properly. Delorme could keep the cow until it had two calves as long as he looked after her. A. Peltier was allowed to keep the treaty oxen for three years, then he had to hand them over to another Indian.[23]

All together, the Crooked Lake Agency Indians had 414 head of privately owned livestock and 509 government animals, including 34 sheep. They sold 57 head that year, killed 40 for beef, and 20 died accidentally.[24]

They had some trouble with disease. Two native[25] horses were diagnosed with glanders[26] and were shot. They burned the carcasses and disinfected the stables to avoid any further contamination.

The agent wintered a pedigree Galloway cow, which had a heifer calf, and Ochapowace had a red pedigree Durham bull.

The Indians dug a well on Kahkewistahaw but hit quicksand when they tried to drill on Ochapowace and had to quit. They drilled with horses back then, and they didn't have the equipment to get through quicksand.

All the Crooked Lake Agency farmers combined seeded twenty more acres that year than the one before. Their farming practices were getting better, especially when it came to preparing the land for planting. They put ninety-five acres into summer fallow and seeded sixty-four acres to oats. The agent seeded another seven acres of oats on summer fallow. That crop was used to feed the agency team of horses.[27]

You would think the government would be pleased at how the Indians took to farming after such a short period of time. It was only a few years ago they were hunting the buffalo. But I guess the Indians weren't learning quite fast enough. This is what was written in the sessional papers:

> Every year shows that these Indians, at any rate, are realizing the fact that it pays them better to mind their own business, and stay at home, instead of so much visiting, which was the great drawback a few years ago. It is by no means as it should be yet, but our motto is, and must be, patience. The greatest trouble I have in this respect is the dairying interest. Many Indians start in the spring, when the cows calve, to become butter makers, but something takes them away for a few days (not necessarily off the reserve) and the interest flags, and then they get word that some relative on another reserve is sick and they must visit the sick one at any cost and, if restrained, they give up their efforts and get sulky, but, exceptions prove the rule and there is a marked advance this summer. One Indian woman came and asked me to lend her some old butter tubs, as she has already some sixty pounds stored away for winter and is going on still, and there will be a few more who will have all the butter they want for the winter. There are four new milk houses put up this summer and one of them on a large scale. If this increases, I shall have to turn my attention to the question of cold storage as the Indians could easily make two thousand, or more, pounds of butter if it suited them to apply themselves in that direction. I am leading up to this, but, as the department is aware, it is lost labor to drive an Indian.[28]

Some of the people who moved to Crooked Lake with Little Child were getting old. By 1896, there were twelve old people who were totally destitute and had to be cared for.[29]

Most reserve children went to school. There were 78 pupils from Crooked Lake Agency in various schools: 8 went to the Regina Industrial School, 41 were at Fort Qu'Appelle Industrial, 9 at Elkhorn Industrial School, and 20 at Round Lake Indian Boarding School. In all, there were 180 school-age children on the reserves, including those who were considered infirm and the 40 from Sheesheep's band (a part of Sakimay) whose parents would not allow them to attend school.[30]

Several families from Sakimay, Kahkewistahaw, Ochapowace, and Cowessess wanted to move their children to the school at Round Lake and presented a petition to the Indian agent to get the number of students who could attend that school increased. That school was a different religious denomination and the agent would not hear of moving children from one school to another. Besides, he didn't want the parents to think they could have any opportunity to interfere. "The chief argument against allowing more children to be sent to Round Lake is that they are so liable to be interfered with by the parents."[31]

The reserves were supposed to be dry—no liquor allowed—but about this time, a homesteader who was making a bit of moonshine found a market for his product on the reserve. He and the Indians he supplied were arrested and sent to prison. That was supposed to discourage anyone else from running liquor. This is how the incident was written up in the Sessional Papers of 1896.

> A Swede had introduced whisky into their teepee, whilst camped near Broadview. The Swede and Indians implicated were arrested, and I tried them, in conjunction with Mr. Holson, J.P., and sentenced them to various terms of imprisonment. As this is the first case of the kind, I trust it will be the last. I think the warning to Indians and settlers will be beneficial.[32]

The Crooked Lake Agency kept winning prizes at the fairs and agriculture shows. At the Regina exhibition, the Indians entered over one hundred exhibits; seventy were women's work, including cheese and soap. The farm instructor's wife, Mrs. Sutherland, had been teaching fancywork to the Indian women. They got first and second prize for fancy sewing, women's clothing, and men's suits and second prize for the best collection of vegetables. The Indians also won first and second prizes for wheat, first and second for oats and for bread, and first for butter.

McDonald managed to get a steam engine for the reserves. He cut a deal with Massey-Harris to supply equipment. When he wrote his report, McDonald noted an improvement in the cleanliness and living situation of the reserve, due mainly, he said, to the training the Indian girls received at school.

> This is appreciable due to the presence of daughters home from school. Some of these girls have very lately married, and I hope in my next annual report to go fully into this matter. The gardens of this agency, both Indians' and employees', are superb; I have never seen them better, and they are a sight well worth seeing. Some of the Indian gardens are well laid out, weeded and kept, and there is a most decided improvement this year in this respect. The great difficulty is to get the Indians to understand how necessary it is to thin out the young growing plants, to give the others room to grow, but they are every year appreciating the value of garden produce more than formerly.[33]

The Cowessess band had good houses, stables, and fences. It was in a central position in the Crooked Lake Agency and had the agency buildings on it, so made more advancements than some of the other nearby reserves.[34]

I wish I'd been around to see the Cowessess Reserve in the way the Department of Indian Affairs described it, especially my relatives' homes and farms.

Chief Nepapheness, who was known by Treaty 2, had a fine homestead with a one-and-a-half storey house, 20 by 14 feet (6 x 4 m), with a thatched roof and a lean-to kitchen, whitewashed outside and in and well furnished. A large picture of the queen hung along with others on the wall. He had a mower, binder, and rake, two wagons, a democrat, buckboard, two bobsleighs, hayracks, a land roller, and heavy and light harness. There were five Canadian horses on his place (three he had raised himself), three colts, hens and pigeons, a storehouse and granary, eight bags of flour and 60 bushels of wheat, bran, and shorts (the product of his own gristing), a horse stable, curry-combs and brushes, a 38-by-16 foot (12 x 5 m) cattle shed for young stock, a cattle stable with stalls and mangers and calf compartments, a henhouse, and an implement shed. He had potatoes on hand, hauled hay twelve miles (19 km), had cut and hauled one thousand rails the past winter for new fences, and had a twenty-acre field in the valley. Nepapheness had seven head of government cattle and six private, all in excellent condition. Plenty of hay and water were easily obtained. "This is a fine place," wrote the Indian agent, "and would put many a

This sturdy settlers' home was dug several feet into the ground. Tom and Mattie Sefton built this poplar pole–and–mud house about five miles (1 km) north of the Cotham School. Bert Sefton personal collection

white farmer to shame."[35]

Equequanape had a 21-by-21-foot (6.5 x 6.5 m) house with an open chimney. The women were sewing and ironing. He had an interest in a binder, had a wagon, mower, and rake, two bobsleighs, and double harness. His son had seven hens and five horses. "There is a stable with eleven stanchions, slab floor, is good and warm and has a spring nearby. He has seven head of cattle, three private, nine sheep and four lambs. A boy and girl have just come home from the Qu'Appelle School."[36]

Aisaican had a well-furnished house, 21 by 25 feet (6.5 x 7.5 m), with a thatched roof and rooms upstairs. He had twenty-five bushels of potatoes for seed. His daughter had just returned from Qu'Appelle School and was doing good work in the house and made butter. There were good stables, a sheep house and henhouse, with a spring at the foot of the hill, close to the stables. Aisaican had made a land roller and wooden shovels. He had two oxen, six sheep, and seven head of private cattle. It was "altogether a thrifty, tidy looking place."[37]

Baptiste Henry (or Henri) had a larger house, 19 by 19 feet (6 x 6 m), with a lean-to used as a storehouse and an upstairs. He had a half-interest in a binder, owned the usual implements and furnishings, made butter in the summer and packed enough for winter use. Henry raised three head of government cattle and ten private.[38]

Zach and Marie LeRat's home, built in the 1920s, was a modern structure for the time. It measured about 20 by 20 feet (6 x 6 m) with one big room on the main floor and an upstairs that could hold several beds. It was built of logs, had a lumber roof, shingles, and a wood floor instead of dirt. Harold LeRat personal collection.

Kanaswaywetung had a large house, 20 by 21 feet (6 x 6.5 m), with an open chimney but a fancy stove. There was fancy needlework around. He had no field yet; he was a hunter and had no cattle. A very fine map hung on the wall, made by his son at Qu'Appelle School. The children were well dressed and perfectly clean and the wife a good housekeeper.[39]

Ambrose Delorme had a double house with one wood and one mud floor and was building a new house. He had stoves, beds, tables and chairs; a binder, mower, and rake, and other articles all under cover; twenty bags of potatoes and some turnips in a root house; nine head of cattle; a good well, a henhouse, and cattle and horse stables. Delorme was described as "a thrifty man and has a comfortable place."[40]

Norbert Delorme lived in a 14-by-14-foot (4 x 4 m) house with an open chimney. It was the only house on the reserve without a wooden floor; the floor was covered with the matting off tea chests. The floor and house was as clean as a new pin. "This man works a good deal round the agency, when the interpreter is absent on the reserve."[41]

Alex Gaddie was also a very successful farmer, with a 20-by-20-foot (6 x 6 m) house with upstairs rooms and a thatched roof, well furnished with stoves, beds, clocks, mirrors, and ornaments. He owned a binder, two bobsleighs, five hayracks, a wagon, a buckboard, heavy double harness, two mowers and rakes, a plough, land roller, a counter scale, milk strainers, and churn (all private property). He had eight Canadian mares, horses, and colts and three native horses; some were splendid specimens. He had a dairy and made good butter. The storehouse had thirty-one bags of flour in it, his own gristing; he sold flour to others of the band at $2.50 a bag. The granary was well filled with wheat and oats for seed and for sale. It was noted that in one day he took two wagons loaded with wheat to sell in Broadview. There was also a new stable with twelve stanchions; a henhouse and twelve hens; a shed for young stock; a second cattle stable with eight stanchions, a slab floor, and a quantity of straw in a stack and hay. A spring of water ran near the buildings. Gaddie had a good garden and a calf pasture.

> The farm boasted two splendid teams of horses, good harness and wagons, the whole showing a lively picture of an industrious Indian. The best made hay stack I have seen in the Territories was here. I did not compliment him on the large manure piles. He said he would have them hauled out to the fields. He has a box stove obtained in the old days from the Hudson's Bay Company, and it cost him $75. It is a solid stove and would weigh as much as a half a dozen of those modern ones. It came by Hudson Bay and York Factory. This is a thriving homestead and Mr. Gaddie is generally successful in having good crops.

He had a lot of land ready for seed, with twenty-three head of private cattle, "looking well, they had the run of the straw stacks in the day time all winter."[42]

Zach LeRat had a house that measured 20 by 18 feet (6 x 5.5 m).

> It was clean with an open chimney, cookstove, wood floor, two beds, one black walnut, four chairs, cupboard, and water barrel. The house was whitewashed inside, had pictures and a good supply of small implements and tools, a bob sleigh, wagon, two racks, a mower and rake and a set of double harness. They made butter and had tins and dishes, all clean. There was a storehouse 16 by 14 [feet (5 x 4 m)] for implements and harness. Le Rat had five horses, poultry and a good horse stable, cattle stable with five stanchions and two large stalls, two head of government cattle and 16 head of private stock, all looking well. Also a corral for calves and a good spring close to the house.[43]

Joe LeRat had a house 20 by 20 feet (6 x 6 m) with the usual furniture. He had three horses, four head of cattle, and good stable with stanchions. "The best contrivance of a stable door I saw here; the man is handy with tools."[44]

Mrs. LeRat had a 14-by-14-foot (4 x 4 m) house with six head of private cattle.

Ambroise LeRat had a 15-by-15-foot (4.5 x 4.5 m) house with a black walnut bedstead. He was just beginning farming, and lived with his mother with no cattle.[45]

Wapamouse had no house but seven horses, a fair stable, and six head of cattle.[46]

Ed Peltier lived in a house 16 by 16 feet (5 x 5 m), well furnished, and had six head of cattle.[47]

Aug. Peltier had a neat house, 16 by 16 feet, with an open chimney, cotton on the walls; also a good stable and spring, hay in the corral, and five head of cattle. "His wife was formerly at Qu'Appelle school and keeps her house very neatly as all the girls from there."[48]

P. Peltier had a 16-by-16-foot house that was being cleaned up. There was an open chimney. He had fifteen bushels of potatoes for seed, made butter, and had five head of private cattle.[49]

H. Peltier had a clean, comfortable, 15-by-14-foot (4.5 x 4 m) house, three sacks of potatoes for seed, one horse, five hens, a mower, two oxen, and one cow.[50]

Joe Peltier and his wife were both Qu'Appelle pupils. Their house measured 18 by 16 feet (5.5 x 5 m) and was well furnished. He had three private cows and two horses. "This boy is anxious to get along and has made a good start."[51]

William Aisaican was a boy from the Qu'Appelle School, a beginner at farming. His wife was also a pupil from Qu'Appelle. He had a small field broken, a new stable building, and logs on the ground for a new house, one horse, five hens, and four head of private cattle, but he still lived with his father-in-law.[52]

Wahpekaneraup "has a snug little place, 14 x 15 [foot (4 x 4.5 m)] house, with an open chimney and clean bedding. He has three horses, twelve hens and potatoes in a pit. There is a small lake and spring near the place. The window and doorframes are painted. He has three head of private cattle."[53]

P. Redmond lived in a double house, 13 by 16 feet (4 x 5 m), with a kitchen on one side. Redmond was a carpenter. He and his wife were just starting out. They had been pupils at the Qu'Appelle Industrial School. The house was nicely furnished with stained sideboard, a

The Crooked Lake Indians of the late 1800s were progressive farmers. The agency owned modern equipment, including a steam engine and threshing machine. Early settlers relied on neighbouring reserves to assist with harvesting. By the early 1940s, some band members owned their own threshing machines. The threshing team went around from farm to farm on the reserve until all the harvesting was complete. If the farmers' fields were on the opposite side of the reserve, the crew would stay with the farm family until the threshing was over. Glenbow Archives (NA2459-5)

bureau, washstand, and bed with covered frame, curtains, a couch, stoves, and tables. Redmond had a tool chest with a good assortment of tools. He had made his own furniture at the school. He had four bags of potatoes for seed, a stable, and four head of private cattle.

There was a small shack opposite his house occupied by an old woman, "but it was closed when we called, the old woman does scrubbing and washing at the agency."[54]

Here is what was said about the O'Soup place:

> This is the homestead formerly occupied by Peter O'Soup's father who was chief of the band for a while. The young man is making good promise of an industrious farmer and is likely to get along well. He has made a good beginning by getting a sensible, thrifty wife. The main house is 20 x 25 [feet (6 x 7.5 m)], divided into two rooms with an upstairs, well furnished and very clean, a kitchen

Iky Taylor, Indian Agent, Crooked Lake. Indian agents were appointed by the government to live on the agency and manage reserve business. They also had some legal powers to hold trials and report Indians to the police. Some agents were fair and decent while others made life difficult on the reserves. The last Indian agent to live on the Crooked Lake Agency moved into Broadview in the 1950s. The Indians then had to go to Broadview to meet with the agent. Broadview Historical and Museum Association (80: 493)

at one end with a good sized hall in the centre, shingled roofs and house whitewashed outside and in; walnut bedsteads, cook stove shining bright. An old house is used as a granary. There is also a small dairy, store house, horse stable, shed, sheep house, piggery, hen house, cattle stable with 12 stanchions and another with seven stanchions and one stall; good fences and 50 acre field fenced in for hay meadow, 64 acres fenced for crops, all implements under cover, hand made land rollers. He has some good pigeons, ten bushels of potatoes for seed, two horses, six head of cattle, hay and straw stacks, and a fine spring of water. Old O'Soup was one of the most enterprising of the band when I was here ten years ago. He has gone to Lake Dauphin to settle.[55]

Sutherland, the farm instructor, had his buildings painted a terra-cotta colour. The house was lined with tarpaper, with lumber on the outside. The mill was close to the house. It turned almost 600 bushels of wheat into over 26,000 pounds of flour that year. The grain separator (threshing machine) was in a shed. It had been working for three seasons and the engine was still in good condition. The staff bought a circular saw for twenty dollars. That saved time and they were able to cut all the wood for the mill and for household use.

The instructor had a cow stable, and the horse shed had room for five horses, a loft for hay and oats, and a spout to feed the oats. There was a carpenter's shop complete with bench and tools. There were ox collars and whittle trees in the shop and lumber on hand to make

them. There was also a blacksmith shop and a neat and well-kept re-
pair shop.[56] Between 1889 and 1896 the band purchased six binders,
ten mowers, seven rakes, eighteen wagons, as well as other smaller
implements and tools.[57]

At band meetings, the Indians sometimes argued over what to do
with money in the band account. Some would suggest to buy cattle or
equipment and others just wanted to leave the cash in the bank.

Alex Gaddie was often the interpreter. The Indians didn't speak
much English and the agent didn't always know Cree or Saulteaux.
The agent made it clear that if the Indians bought cattle they would
not be able to sell the calves when and where they liked. The same
rules would apply as did to treaty cattle. They could not sell any animals without a permit. At one meeting, the Indians tossed the options
around for a couple of hours and decided to buy two disc harrows. No
one voted to buy cattle after hearing that from the agent.

If you were an Indian, you had to get permission for almost anything you wanted to do, from taking a trip to another reserve to selling a load of hay. Indians were not allowed to market their own produce without a permit. If they grew grain or cut wood on the reserve
or raised cattle, they had to get a permit in order to sell it.

The Indian agent was in charge of issuing permits. If you wanted
to buy things off the reserve, like groceries or other supplies, even
clothes, the Indian agent decided whether or not that was allowed.
This law remained in the *Indian Act* until 1995, but by the 1960s it
was pretty much ignored. Indian Affairs knew by then that it was not
right.

The Oblate priests, with Father Theophile Campeau as Superior,
and several nuns took up residence on Cowessess Reserve towards
the end of the 1890s. They called Crooked Lake "Lac Croche." They
built a presbytery (priest's house), and the Sisters of Notre Dame des
Missions de Lyon came from France to take care of the residential
school.

The church, which was called the Sacred Heart of Mary, measured
56 by 20 feet (17 x 6 m) with walls 14 feet (4 m) high. It could hold
two hundred people, and it cost around one hundred dollars to build.
There was a tower and bell and a fenced cemetery close to the church.
In the Sessional Papers they wrote of the mission, "The whole place
reflected credit on the good taste of the Indians and the Rev. Father
Campeau. There is a building for Indians to meet in when visiting,

stables, a new house is to be built for the missionary, in the meantime, and the vestry is occupied. The church is supplied with benches, made by the Indians, and they take care of the church and cemetery."[58]

The rectory was about 30 x 20 feet (9 x 6 m). The sisters lived in there for a while.

The boarding school at Marieval on Cowessess Reserve opened at the end of 1898. Six students attended. There was room for forty-five. The school wasn't finished that fall so work continued over the winter. The school was a big, two-and-a-half-storey structure with a stone basement. It was fully equipped with every modern convenience imaginable, including acetylene lights that worked from a gas engine. There was even running water from a gasoline-powered motor.

The Cowesses Boarding School annual report of 1899 contained the following report on the school:

> I have the honour to submit my report on the Crooked Lake Board-ing School for the year ended June 30, 1898. The school was first opened on December 19, 1898. The structure is not yet completed, therefore we are obliged to carry on the work of the school in build-ings already existing. The school is beautifully situated at the south end of Crooked Lake on Cowesses' Reserve, in the Qu'Appelle Val-ley. The area of land connected with the school is not known. A beautiful and very commodious building, 57 x 37 feet [17 x 11 m], will be completed by next October. It will be three stories high, with a nice basement containing the kitchen, dining-room, pantry, dairy, laundry and a cellar, with sufficient room for furnaces. The new building is frame and will be brick-veneered afterwards.
>
> There will be ample accommodation for forty-five children. The sanitary condition of the new school will be, I believe, all that can be desired. The house will be roomy, bright and very well ventilated.
>
> The attendance during the six months has been very good. We have fourteen children on the roll. Having received no grant from the department last December, our school boarders have been completely supported at the expense of the mission. As the children are all beginners, the class-room work does not extend beyond the first two standards.
>
> Fifteen acres of land are now under cultivation and we have bro-ken up eight acres more during this summer. This spring we put in nearly ten acres of crop and planted thirty bushels of potatoes. We have in the garden onions, lettuce, rhubarb, carrots, beets, parsnips, pease, beans, cucumbers and melons.
>
> The boys are chiefly confined to farming and gardening. The girls are taught domestic work. Every day there is a three-quarters of an hour devoted to religious instruction, after school hours. All the children have enjoyed good health. The sanitary condition of

The Marieval Mission needed a big barn for its livestock and hay. The mission farm kept twenty or more horses for farm work. The farm boss and the boys from the residential school milked between twenty and thirty cows by hand every day, and they kept beef cattle as well. The barn was impressive, complete with slings to pull the hay up into the loft. Harold LeRat personal collection

the surroundings has been carefully attended to. Two wells give us all the water we require. The water is excellent. The present buildings are heated by ordinary stoves. The new school will be heated by "New Idea" furnaces.[59]

Close to the school was a 20-by-30-foot (6 x 9 m) shop and a 20-by-20-foot (6 x 6 m) house for the Indians to stop in before and after mass. The stables were built as an annex to the house and were used for the farm animals.

The congregation and the priests picked up the complete cost for the church presbytery and the school. The Oblates also paid for the upkeep and even the children's clothing that year. The government never contributed to the construction as the band had been promised. They finally came across with a subsidy for the maintenance and boarding fees for twenty students, but not until after the school was up and running.

In those early years, two resident Roman Catholic priests lived at the mission and four sisters stayed at the boarding school.

As the years went by, things changed so much for the Indians, the mission, and the priests, and in religious education for the children. Many of the Indians and Métis became Roman Catholics, but some took to the Protestant church.

The mission in the valley became important to more than just the Indians. Catholics from all over the area came to worship: the Germans from Grayson to the north and Hungarians from Kaposvar to the east, and even some French Canadian families that settled nearby.

Eventually Chief Nepapheness from Cowessess and most of his family became Catholics. Yellow Calf, Sheesheep, and Kahkewistahaw stayed with their traditional beliefs like Little Child and did not accept the church. Gaddie might have become Presbyterian, as church services were held at his house.[60]

O'Soup finally decided to leave the Cowessess reserve, and on June 28, 1898, he requested a transfer to the Pine Creek Reserve in the Treaty 2 area. Everyone present at Cowessess voted in favour of the transfer.[61]

On July 6 of the same year, his son Peter O'Soup also transferred to Pine Creek Reserve.[62] But less than a year later, Peter O'Soup was allowed to rejoin the Cowessess band. His request stated that he had not applied to leave the reserve on his own, and that his father, who had applied for his son, had no authority to transfer on his behalf. Even though the older O'Soup had left the Cowessess reserve, Louis claimed he never stopped being a member of Cowessess band.

Before the turn of the century, the Cowessess Reserve No. 73 totalled almost 50,000 acres. The southern part had some good hay marshes. Weed Creek ran clear through the reserve to the Qu'Appelle Valley through a weedy ravine. There were plenty of trees along the banks, mainly poplar and elm, and there were fish in the river.

Nearly all of the Indians had taken up farming and kept some livestock. Some had as many as twenty or thirty head. They sold firewood and hay. Surplus grain was hauled to Broadview and Grenfell. Beef cattle were sold to the department because, remember, the Indians had to have a permit to sell anything.

Most of their homes were fairly comfortable, mainly made of logs with thatch on the roof. Some had shingles. There were log stables and other outbuildings around. The Sessional Papers of 1899 reported that the stock came from mainly grade[63] cows mixed with shorthorn or Galloway bulls. "The sale of their private animals is discouraged, as much as possible and with care, they will have herds of a good size in a very short time. The Indians are getting together a good lot of improved implements such as binders, seeders, disc harrows and a good stock of ploughs, harrows, sleighs, wagons and smaller implements."[64]

> The majority of these Indians work fairly well at farming and stock-raising, although it has been hard to get them to persevere in their farming operations, the last two seasons having been so poor that

they derived no benefit from their work and were thus naturally discouraged and disinclined to go on working, as they imagined, for nothing. These Indians may all be said to live temperate and moral lives with few exceptions. I have been unable to detect any drunkenness during the year.[65]

There were occasional disagreements between the Indians and the settlers. One time, Zach LeRat wanted to cut hay in an area where he had cut before, but a man named Switzer had also asked the agent if he could put up the hay. Switzer had started to cut it when the band found out. The agent was away, so the Indians told Switzer to stop cutting until the agent came home. They didn't think the agent should give out permits without consulting them first. The band said that either the hay that had been cut should be given to LeRat or they would take it away from Switzer themselves. LeRat offered to compromise and take ten of the twenty-five tons the other guy had cut.

When the agent came back, he sided with Switzer. The agent said he told the settler he could cut at the far corner of the reserve, but only if no one was cutting there. The agent didn't think LeRat would cut that far from his home. In the end, the agent decided that since Switzer had cut about twenty-five tons before he was stopped and since he was already stacking the hay, he should just pay for it and the money would go to the band.

That was the first permit the agent had issued to cut hay on the reserve because they had never had more than they needed before. This year though, the agent told them that there was tons of hay on the reserve that would go to waste and that the band had better be careful because Switzer had a permit and the hay was his property. They could be charged for stealing it. The agent said that he had every right to issue permits without asking the band's permission. He did agree, in the future, not to issue any permits without consulting the band, but stood firm on the fact that the money from the sale of the hay permits was a benefit to the whole band.[66]

Maybe there wasn't as much hay available as the agent wanted the Indians to believe. There was a crop failure from frosts and drought. Only 500 bushels of wheat and 150 bushels of oats were harvested. Alex Gaddie had the best yield, but from 75 acres he threshed only 300 bushels of wheat and 60 of oats.[67]

5
Stolen Land, Broken Promises

The new century rolled in, and the agent was still calling a lot of the shots when it came to elections. Sometimes he would even break a tie during a vote, even though the agents were not band members. They should not have had a vote in an Indian election.

The usual custom in a band election was to have the chief elected first and then the men who had not been elected could run for headmen if they wanted. The agent said this was not the way it was supposed to be done because "he would have to sit an hour to receive the nominations for chief, then hold the election, then receive nominations for one hour for headmen, then hold the election. This course would take more time."[1]

The band decided to hold the elections separately. The agent said each candidate could appoint one man as scrutineer to stay in the room during the voting to look after his interests and speak to it later if there were any objections.

When it came time for the election, the room was cleared and the voters came back in one at a time to vote. Nepapheness won against Gaddie by one vote, nine to eight. Joseph LeRat also had eight votes, and Zach LeRat had three. Alex Gaddie was nominated for headman but refused and withdrew from the contest.[2]

Joseph LeRat received twenty-four votes and was elected, as was J. B. Sparvier with fourteen. Sometimes the process used is hard to figure out. This time, more votes were recorded for headmen than for chief. Maybe people were late and only got there in time to vote for the headmen.

Two of the four candidates for chief voted for themselves. Nepapheness voted for Zach LeRat, but Zach voted for Joseph LeRat. Alex

Gaddie and Joseph LeRat voted for themselves. It was obviously not a secret ballot.

After a serious discussion about the vote, the band broke from talk of politics to discuss the sports day to be held on Friday, July 20.[3] They decided to make the track for the horse racing on July 13.

Chief Nepapheness built a new house and stables around this time and gave the old farmstead to his son-in-law.[4]

In 1901, the elder Pierre LeRat, who was known by Treaty Number 11, with the Indian name of Pitawewekijik, came back to his home on the Cowessess Reserve. He'd been living in the United States at Turtle Mountain in North Dakota continuously since 1888, but had never been given permission to go south. One of his wives and two children died there.

The Indian agent wrote to the department to ask for LeRat to be paid his annuity for 1901 and commented that he was old and blind and would live with his brother. It is not likely that he lived with his brother. If I'm correct about the family history, Pitawewekijik's brother Francis died back at Turtle Mountain. The old man would likely have lived with one of his sons, either Zach or Pierre Jr. The last time Pitawewekijik had been mentioned on the pay list was in 1887, but he did not ask for back pay.

This is how Magnus Begg, the Indian agent, explained it in his letter to Indian Affairs on August 19, 1901:

> I have the honour to acknowledge receipt of Department letter of above date [July 30, 1901] relative to the request of Pierre LeRat to be allowed to rejoin Cowessess Band; and in reply to state that this man has resided continuously since 1888 at Turtle Mountain Reserve in the United States and never left for further south as other Indians have done. He had only his wife and two children who have died there. He had no permission from the Superintendent General to reside in the United States. As he was alone he returned here to his brother who will not let him leave as he is so old and blind being about 80 years of age, so that if the Department grants his request he cannot draw Treaty very long.[5]

The department agreed to the request and allowed him to be paid annuities for 1901, with no arrears.[6] Pitawewekijik lived for quite a few years after he came back to Canada, until around 1911.

The Cowessess band totalled 160 people at the start of the twentieth century.[7] Some of the people on the reserve were half-breeds, Métis. Back then, the Indians were put on reserves and got the annual

$5 treaty payment, but the half-breeds did not get reserves and were not paid annuities. They could apply for scrip.

Scrip was issued to half-breeds because they had Indian blood and had also lost their land. Scrip was really just a piece of paper that could be turned into money to be used to buy land. Some half-breeds didn't buy land with their scrip; they sold it for a fraction of what it was worth to speculators who then bought up huge tracts of land.

Some half-breeds who were living on the reserve didn't want to take scrip; they were more interested in being admitted to treaty. Agent Wright wrote a letter to the Indian commissioner to ask if certain young half-breeds who had married treaty women could be allowed to join treaty instead of taking scrip. The answer was that they could not get treaty.

That's interesting because the government had given treaty to Métis before, like Gaddie. That is how Indian Affairs did things: give only certain ones treaty, and some they said no. This time, though, the response was that there was no law to allow non-treaty men to enter treaty; any half-breed living on the reserve was trespassing.[8]

They also discussed whether half-breeds now in treaty could leave treaty and take scrip. The agent read them the commissioner's circular letter of October 7, 1899, which stated that mixed bloods would not be allowed to leave treaty.

The government changed its mind about half-breeds living on reserves and decided that if they were living on reserve as Indians that they should be given treaty instead of scrip. One of the concerns was whether that meant half-breeds who had already received their scrip.

In 1890, Pierre LeRat Jr. was discharged from treaty and given scrip totalling $160 because his wife was entitled to scrip as a Métis. It is a bit confusing because both my great-grandfather and his son were called Pierre LeRat. Pierre's father, Pitawewekijik, and Pierre's brother Zach (my grandfather) stayed in treaty.

Zach's brother Pierre and his wife, Cecile Desjarlais, lived on Cowessess and worked for Zach for a couple years before Pierre decided to request that his family be allowed back into treaty.

Even though there were bureaucrats that did not agree with allowing half-breeds into treaty, the deal ended up that if the half-breeds came back into treaty, their annual treaty money for all members of the family would be held back until the amount paid to them in scrip was recovered. Those who didn't agree would keep their scrip and should leave the reserve.

In the case of Pierre LeRat and his wife, the minister gave permission for them to take treaty if they paid back the scrip out of their treaty annuity payments. When it was cleared up, the family could once again collect treaty payments.[9]

The total amount that was to be refunded out of treaty annuities was $160, the value of the half-breed scrip they had received in 1890.

Pierre's formal written acceptance to take treaty in the Cowessess Band for himself and his wife and children was acknowledged and the Indian agent sent the first payment of $35 back to the department.[10] It must have taken quite a few years to pay back the $160 at $35 a year, and then there was no treaty money to buy any of the things the family needed.

There was a list of fourteen half-breeds from the area that wanted to take treaty. About half of the band members on Cowessess were in favour of allowing the half-breeds to take treaty; the other half were against. The department officials made mention that the ones against were the best workers.

Mr. Begg, the agent, didn't like the idea of the half-breeds returning to the reserve. He argued that most of them had already received scrip and for the most part were a worthless lot who would not work themselves and discouraged the Indians from working.[11] He didn't want to make an exception for the two men he thought were different from the others, so he recommended against anyone being admitted.

The commissioner agreed with the agent. "From my experience of Halfbreeds readmitted into Treaty I do not consider that they improve their position very much by returning to the reserve for they are generally a worthless lot of people who will not work and very often discourage the Indians from doing so. I therefore recommend that the applications be not entertained."[12]

Some of the applicants had decent assets: wagons, harness, pigs, cattle, horses, ploughs, binders, and sleighs, but they didn't have a chance if the agent didn't think they were the right sort.

Charles Peltier had a treaty wife, a four-year-old boy and a two-year-old girl. They had twelve head of cattle, fourteen horses, three pigs, ten poultry, two ploughs, two wagons, a binder, mower, democrat, sleigh, buggy, and harrows.

Roger White, who had taken scrip twenty-five years previous, had a wife in treaty, a three-year-old and a four-month-old daughter, seven head of cattle, four horses, a pig, binder, mower, and set of sleighs.

Jos Leduc, an American half-breed with only one arm, was also

Magnus Begg was the Indian agent at Crooked Lake around 1900. The agency house in the photo was typical of the time. The agent moved his family to the reserve and lived like most of the settlers in the area. He had a modern home and good outbuildings: a chicken coop, a pigsty, and a large hip-roof barn for cattle and horses. The agent's family milked cows and had a big garden. Glenbow Archives (NA-867-5)

refused. His wife had taken scrip two years previously. Leduc had two ponies, a wagon, sleigh, harness, and four girls and two boys.[13] I think this might have been Joseph Nadeau and they just misspelled his name. Nadeau was married to my grandfather Zach's sister Suzanne. Nadeau had only one arm and came to Canada about that time and then went back to the States. There could not have been too many people around with only one arm.

That Indian agent, Magnus Begg, was new to the job, so I don't know how he knew anything about the people who applied. The Indians thought the previous agent, Mr. Wright, worked them too hard sometimes, but they seemed to like him well enough. Then along came Begg, who even wanted to change the sports day activities. After treaty payment, the Indians liked to get together and do some horse racing. Begg thought they should have an exhibition instead and compete for prizes for the best-kept gardens, field houses, cattle, sheep, pigs, and poultry, and the women should enter their needlework, knitting, bread, and butter, more like exhibitions in neighbouring towns.

Government assistance under the ration system was eliminated about this time. No able-bodied person was to get any relief without working for it. The only exceptions were old women and those who were crippled and could not work.

I believe my mother was born in 1902. The Oblates brought her to the reserve as a little baby. The priests sometimes went to the mission at Lebret and returned to the reserve with abandoned children who they gave to the Indians to raise. The children were readily accepted and raised as Indians.

Two or three babies ended up on the Crooked Lake reserves Kah-kewistahaw, Sakimay, and Cowessess. O'Soup adopted one of the children, the McKay family another, and the Peltiers took in my mother. The priests named her Madeleine, but she was called Mariah.

I found out that my mother was not a treaty Indian when I went to school. Some of the kids would call us white, or blue-eyed Indians. My sisters thought my mother had been brought out from Winnipeg, but I think she came from Qu'Appelle. Her father was supposed to be a wealthy merchant and her mother the maid, or that is how the story goes. She was illegitimate, and the priests had to find her a home.

Gus Peltier and Annie Two Voice (who was the daughter of Kanas-waywetung) adopted the baby and raised her. Gus and Annie were

Solomon LeRat, 1920s. Harold LeRat personal collection

Mariah LeRat (Harold's mother) with farm hitch, early 1930s. Harold LeRat personal collection

listed as Augustin Peltier and Annie Kanijiwilang or Kenywiwtang in different records.

My mother became a Peltier and went to school on Cowessess with my father, Solomon LeRat. They got married and had eight children.

I was only four and my younger brother Gordon was a newborn when mother died. My father died the next year. My oldest brother, George, raised me. He was only twenty and just newly married when our parents died. My oldest sister, Florence, raised Gordon.

A few years ago, I was looking through some of the church records at the mission and found a record of my parents' wedding. The way it was written in the mission's family book was that Mariah was adopted and then in brackets, in French, was the name Coupal and the word *father*. The priest must have known who her father was and wrote the name in the book. Some man with the last name of Coupal was my grandfather. Over the years, I put together a couple of theories but never found any solid connection to family on my mother's side.

It was hard to find out anything more because the priests' records were so bad. When I went to get married, I found I was listed as Arnold. I actually had a different name. I have always gone by the name Harold, but because the priests were French and couldn't pronounce the "H," I guess they thought I was Arnold.

Now the church records have disappeared.

Maybe we will never really know that side of the family tree. But it just shows how welcome children were on the reserve, whether they were Indian, Métis, or white, it didn't matter. My mother needed a home. The priests brought her to the reserve and Gus and Annie welcomed that baby, brought her up lovingly. Gus was the only grandfather I knew. My other grandfather, Zach LeRat, died in 1930.

The people around Broadview and Whitewood were at it again, trying to get rid of the Indians. It was less than twenty years since they took up the first petition to move the reserves further north. This time the idea was to get the Indians to surrender the whole south half of the Crooked Lake reserves, the part closest to the towns, so the land could be sold to settlers; more and more settlers were moving west and wanted farm land.

The commissioner had already brought up the possibility of surrendering a two- or three-mile (3–5 km) strip nearest the railway. The Indians were not interested. Some of the best land on Ochapowace Reserve Number 71 and Kahkewistahaw Number 72 and the best wood was in that area. No wonder the settlers wanted to get their hands on it.

The plan was to sell the land for the best possible price, by the quarter section, at auction, with no restrictions on how much an individual could buy and with no settlement duties involved.

Chief Kahkewistahaw was right when, at the time of treaty, he said that he would take a reserve but that he was pretty sure the government would try to take it back.

A petition was signed by 184 residents of the village of Broadview, the town of Whitewood, and surrounding districts stating that having the reserves so close to the towns seriously retarded their development. The petition also pointed out that the reserves occupied 285 square miles (738 km), which was much more than the current Indian population of six hundred needed. They also stated that there were no Indians living within three miles (5 km) of the southern boundary of the reservation and that they were not using that strip of land for farming or for hunting. Settlers, on the other hand, would contribute to the economic development of the town.[14]

Just as the settlers were hoping to buy the reserve land, Kanaswaywetung, who had been chief at Cowessess for a couple of years in the early 1890s and was also known as Two Voice, asked the Indian agent for a pass so he could go to Winnipeg and apply to purchase a location ticket. His idea was to buy his own plot of land on the southwest corner of the reserve, on the piece of land the settlers were after. He thought that if he lived there, it might stop the sale. It didn't work. He didn't get a location ticket and was considered to be nothing more than a troublemaker. "He wants to interview the proper official here regarding obtaining a plot of land, on reserve, which I understand has not yet been surveyed into towns. The old Indian cannot have his wishes made known without going to Winnipeg and if you can arrange, you will be helping him very materially in arranging the affair in question."[15]

> The Indian is strongly Opposed to selling part of the reserve and as a means to stop this he thinks he can by locating on the extreme South west corner of the reserve. he came to me for a location ticket to locate at once. I told him the corse [sic] to get a ticket to locate on land that the govt subdivided for that purpose. he did not want that. this Indian lives by sale of wood. Their [sic] is no wood or water where he wants to locate it is not surveyed. I may say that this Indian has been a source of trouble alon [sic] this line before. File 38 in this office is exclusively devoted to his previous corospondence [sic] and complaints. I got a good interpreter to explain to him as I expected he would write you on the above. This is all the trouble with this man.[16]

Kanaswaywetung was told that a location ticket could not be issued for any subdivided lands.[17]

As of July 3, 1906, Ochapowace Reserve No. 71 contained 52,864 acres with 102 members; Kahkewistahaw No. 72 contained 46,720 acres for 84 members, and Cowessess No. 73 had 49,920 acres for 173 members. Cowessess had 4 men and 5 women over sixty-five; 28 men and 37 women who were between twenty-one and sixty-five; 7 males and 9 females aged sixteen to twenty; 26 boys and 20 girls between six and fifteen; and there were 17 boys and 20 girls under six.[18]

While all the planning was going into the large surrender, the Indians refused to release a small amount of land for a roadway from the steel bridge crossing the Qu'Appelle on section 4-19-5 west of second meridian. Chief Joe LeRat spoke for the band and said that they had been promised a roadway that would be surveyed where it was to their best advantage. The Indians had picked out a direct road to what was called Aisaican's Hill, but the direction was changed to Nepapheness Hill, which was not as good. It ran along the east side of the reserve, and most of the Indians lived on the west side.[19]

The surveyors agreed that the road could be made on either hill, but the agent didn't. He was worried about getting the engine down Aisaican's Hill. The Indians would not budge and said they would only sign if the road was built out of the valley either by Aisaican's or O'Soup's hill, heading south, close to the agency and keeping as far away as possible from fields or fences that could be damaged by the building of a road. The agent noted, "They will not sign release for the present survey, as it is not as they were promised."[20]

At the same time, it was starting to look like the Indians might change their minds about surrendering their 95,000 acres.[21] Word had reached Crooked Lake that the Pasqua Band had surrendered land and got a good cash payment.

Even the priest seemed to be in on it and was of the opinion that a surrender was possible if things were handled properly with the Indians. The people in the surrounding towns who wanted the surrender had been talking to the leaders on the reserves and had given them all kinds of ideas. When Pasqua was discussing the terms of surrender, the public around Fort Qu'Appelle was not involved and didn't know much about the surrender until it was a done deal. The supporters of the surrender decided it would be best to have the townspeople back off. They also thought a fair price would be three dollars per acre for Ochapowace land and five dollars for Kahkewistahaw and Cowessess. The first one-tenth of the sales proceeds would be paid immediately after the sale.[22]

It was necessary to explain the terms carefully so the department didn't have to go back with a second deal. They had to make sure the person handling the surrender had the ability to meet some of the smaller demands during the meeting and get things locked down right from the start.

Negotiations for surrender were underway early in 1907. Inspector Graham and the Indian agent first met with Cowessess band members on January 21 to explain the terms.[23] Some believe there was no vote at that meeting, but I disagree. I say there were twenty-eight who voted and it was a tie. Peter Houri (farm instructor) was the interpreter. Gaddie was not there.

Gaddie's land was part of the surrender; he farmed a long way from the mission where the meetings were held, out on the southwest corner of the reserve near Oakshella (where the CPR took land from the reserve). Gaddie was not at the first meeting on January 21, but then the Indian agent got together with the priest and said they should get

Joseph LeRat, Cowessess chief. Joe LeRat was the son of Pitawewekijik and brother to Zach. He was considered the leader on Cowessess during the time of the land surrender of 1907, but he was not in favour of selling the land. Alex Gaddie, who had joined Little Child's band as an interpreter in the 1870s and was given Indian status by the agent in 1881, was brought in as interpreter during the final negotiations of the surrender. Gaddie's X is on the surrender documents instead of the chief's. Saskatchewan Archives (A253-5)

Gaddie and offer him improvements for his land and convince him to come to the next meeting and vote yes to the surrender.

After the January 21 meeting, the Indian agent went up to Alex Gaddie's and promised him good money for the improvements he had made on his farm if he would come out and vote for the surrender at the next meeting, to be held a week later on January 29. The agent also got the priest to go and talk to the Indians to try to convince them to sign the surrender at the next meeting. The priest had influence over most of the Indians—maybe not Gaddie, but others.

Why would the agent have gone all the way out to Gaddie's to convince him to come out to vote the following week if there had not been a tie vote at the first meeting?

Alex Gaddie replaced Peter Houri as the interpreter at the January 29 meeting. According to minutes of the meeting, there were twenty-nine voters. The vote was a fourteen-to-fourteen tie. Gaddie broke the tie in favour of surrender.[24]

There were many things that were not right with the surrender. On a surrender agreement, the chief is supposed to sign, or put his mark. On the Cowessess document it should have been Joe LeRat who signed; he was chief. Instead, they wrote Alexander Gaddie's name in the space meant for the chief, stroked out the word "Chief," and wrote "an Indian" to describe Gaddie. This is how the agreement read, as best it can be made out. Hand-written entries on the original are in italics.

Dominion of Canada
Province of *Saskatchewan*
~~County~~ of *Judicial District of Eastern Assiniboia*
To Wit: the _____ of _____

Personally appeared before me,
William M Graham Inspector of Indian Agencies of Qu'Appelle
in the Province of *Saskatchewan*
and *Alexander Gaddie an Indian* ~~Chief~~ of the said Band of Indians
mentioned in the (annexed) release or surrender
AND the said *William M Graham* for Himself saith:

That the annexed release or surrender was assented to by a majority of the male members of the said Band of Indians of the Cowessess Reserve Number 73 of the full age of twenty-one years then present.

That such assent was given at a meeting or council of the said Band summoned for that purpose and according to its Rules.

That he was present at such meeting or council and heard such assent given.

That he was duly authorised to attend such council or meeting by the Superintendent General of Indian Affairs.

That no Indian was present or voted at said council or meeting who was not a member of the Band or interested in the land mentioned in the said Release or Surrender.

And the said *Alexander Gaddie in himself says:* That the annexed Release or Surrender was assented to by him and a majority of the male members of the said Band of Indians of the full age of twenty-one years then present.

That such assent was given at a meeting or council of the said Band of Indians summoned for that purpose, according to its Rules, and held in the presence of the said *Alexander Gaddie.*

That no Indian was present or voted at such council or meeting who was not a habitual resident on the Reserve of the said Band of Indians or interested in the land mentioned in the said Release or Surrender.

That he is a ~~Chief~~ *Indian* of the said Band of Indians and entitled to vote at the said meeting or council.

Sworn before me by the (unknown word) Deponents William M. Graham and Alexander Gaddie
At the town of Moosomin in the County Province of Saskatchewan this Second day of February A.D., 1907.
W. M. Graham
His X
Alexander Gaddie
Mark

The same having been first read over and explained by me to said Alexander Gaddie who seemed to understand the same and made his mark thereto in my presence.

E. L. Wetmore A Justice of the Superior Court of the North-West Territories[25]

Gaddie should not have signed the surrender. He was not even a headman at the time. He was the interpreter. He came to the reserve as a carpenter, building log houses, and stayed.

A list of those Indians present at the surrender was included with the minutes of the meeting, but it doesn't seem right. I believe there were thirty-eight or thirty-nine eligible voters on the reserve, and there were thirty-one men who showed up for the January 29 meeting. When the vote was held, there were twenty-nine names on the list of those who voted. But when it came to the payment, there were twenty-two names listed in agreement with the surrender. Of those who originally voted against the surrender, only five signed the agreement for surrender; nine did not sign.[26]

Francis Delorme and Norbert Delorme were not recorded as having voted either for or against the surrender, but they had their names on the agreement. Another person who supposedly voted yes was Nap Delorme, but he was not even on the reserve. In fact, no one ever knew anyone named Nap Delorme—there was no such person.

In the end, after Gaddie voted for the surrender, the vote was fourteen no and fifteen yes. For a surrender to pass, 50 percent plus one (of eligible voters) had to vote in favour.

If thirty-eight or even thirty-nine could have voted, they would have needed at least twenty votes for the surrender to have a majority, and that didn't happen: there were only fifteen votes in favour.

That is my point: the officials just did what they wanted. They decided that Gaddie could sign the surrender instead of the chief, and then the numbers just don't add up.

To add to all that, when it came time to make the payments, the agent only had permission to pay out thirty-three dollars per person. He didn't have the authority to do it, but he paid double the amount. Because he could not make just one payment of sixty-six dollars, it took twice as long. He had to make two thirty-three-dollar payments. It took half the night to get everybody their money.

Indians who did not vote for the surrender must have showed up to collect the money, and they were the names recorded. Saying no once in Indian society at the time meant no forever, so once that was said, there was no reason to repeat it by showing up to vote again. The Indians believed that keeping silent still meant a no vote. However, by not voting, the opposite happened, and those who voted for surrender got their way.

Some of the Indians didn't go to the meetings because they were against selling the land. The Tanner boys used to say that their dad told them he would not go to the meetings about surrender because he was not in agreement with selling the land. On the recorded notes from the meeting, it says that Alex Tanner was there but he never collected his money. If he had been there, he would likely have collected his $66 because that was a lot of money.

I'd say there were at least fourteen people on the list for collecting the payments who did not vote.

The surrender was final on February 2, 1907, when William Graham put his name next to the Gaddie's "X" stating that the majority of male members over twenty-one of the Cowessess Reserve No. 73 had agreed to the annexation. Then they added a note that Gaddie seemed to understand and had made his mark.[27] It doesn't seem right to me.

According to the agreement of January 29, 1907, the Cowessess Reserve No. 73 would surrender 20,704 acres lying south of the road allowance between projected townships 17 and 18, range 6, west of the second meridian.[28]

Meetings of the same type were held at other reserves. Ochapowace Reserve Number 71 held a meeting on January 22 with twenty-four Indians present. Twenty voted against the surrender.[29] The next day at McKay's mission church, the Kahkewistahaw Reserve Number 72 had nineteen voting Indians present; fourteen voted against.[30]

Five days later, on January 28, 1907, the officials were back at Kahkewistahaw, at the request of a letter signed by a number of voting members of the band and addressed to Inspector Graham asking to hold another meeting to consider of the agreement for surrender. Some of the members had not completely understood the conditions and wanted to change their votes. Seventeen Indians were present. The vote went in favour of surrender eleven to six.[31]

On February 9, 1907, Graham and his officials were back for a meeting at Ochapowace to reconsider surrender. This too was at the request of some band members. Twenty-four were present, and after Graham explained the terms of the proposed surrender nineteen still voted against the surrender.[32]

Miller, the Indian agent, figured there were too many people talking to the Crooked Lake Indians about the surrender and that was why they would not agree to it. He wanted the missionaries to work on the Indians.

The Catholic priests had something to gain from the surrender. They wanted a portion of the valley for themselves. Did the Catholic priests sway the surrender by writing the letters asking for additional meetings to reconsider the vote, or was there an Indian present who could read and write?

Whoever had a hand in making the surrender happen, for whatever reason, it was not a good deal for the Indians. It took years before the reserves were able to recover what they had given up, and you never really get back what is lost.

Shortly after the surrender, Minister of the Interior Frank Oliver was sent a letter on behalf of the Board of Trade of the Town of Broadview, thanking him for his assistance in opening up a portion of the Crooked Lake Reserve adjacent to the town. The letter said that the hard work of Indian Agent Miller and Inspector Graham was much appreciated.

Miller himself purchased the northeast quarter, section 21, township 17, range 5, west of the second meridian for eight dollars per acre. He had previously bought the west half of section 27. Miller wanted the quarter for his son and bought it at an auction in Broadview. He didn't even look at the parcel, just assumed the land was similar to what he already had. When he went out to see what he had bought, he found out he had picked a piece of land that was unsuitable for farming. Miller asked the Department to cancel his purchase of NE 21 and let him pick from some of the other Indian land that had not yet been sold. It seems he did not have the right to purchase the land without permission in the first place.[33] He was in conflict of interest buying that land.

After the surrender, all of the acres Cowessess gave up were sold except one quarter that was under water. That quarter section was leased out for many years and in 1965 the band found out they still had a quarter of land that had not been sold at the time of surrender. After fifty years, the agent said we could lease that quarter out, and we didn't even know that it was Cowessess land.

As if the surrender that winter was not enough, a band meeting was held at Crooked Lake Agency in May for the Indians to consider surrendering land at the boarding school to be used for a mission farm. Inspector Graham planned to pay individuals well for that land. He promised that instead of one-tenth, the Indians would get 50 percent of the purchase price. The other half would go into the band fund and they would get the interest annually. The plan was not to survey unless the Indians voted to surrender. The hay land was not supposed to be part of the two-hundred-acre sale.[34]

Joe LeRat wanted all of the money to be paid up front to the Indians, but Graham said no, only half could be paid and the balance forwarded to the band fund. Alex Gaddie wanted to know if all expenses would be deducted from the $15 per acre payment and Graham said they would. There were twenty-seven Indians present. All voted against the surrender.[35]

The issue came up again in August. The land in question was west of Weed Creek and south of the river. The Roman Catholic mission wanted the land for a farm except for four acres that would be used for a cemetery.

Once again the agent promised to forward 50 percent and distribute 50 percent to the Indians, minus expenses. Twenty-two Indians promised to sign the documents when the agent returned with the papers and the money. Two of those who were willing to sign wanted to keep the hay. That time, Peter LeRat, the chief's brother, was the only vote against the surrender.

The Indians agreed to sell the land to the Oblates for as long as they needed to use it, because they had to feed the children at the school. The government was not helping the school. That way the mission could grow its own grain and raise some cattle. When they didn't need the land anymore, it was supposed to go back to the band.

According to government records, the Oblates bought 323 acres for $4,845, which would have equalled the fifteen dollars an acre the Indians expected when they agreed to the surrender in November 1908. Letters patent were issued to the Oblate Fathers on December 14, 1909.[36]

Fifty percent of the sale price of the land to the Oblate Fathers was distributed to the Indians on a per capita basis before the actual signing of the surrender by the Indians. The remainder of the purchase price was placed in their Capital Trust Account. For all intents and purposes, the Indians at this stage had divested themselves of all interest in the property. You will note that there is no provision in the surrender that the land was to revert to the Indians should the school be abandoned.[37]

In 1925, after the department decided to operate the residential school, the Oblate Fathers sold just over two hundred acres back to the government. The purchase price totalled $70,000, buildings included. The Oblates kept a small parcel of land.[38]

Included in the sale were the Oblate's machinery and animals. The livestock included "four bay mares (11 years old); two bay mares (6 years old); three geldings (8 years old); Two geldings (4 years old); one colt (2 years old); one bay mare (pony); two hackney mares. Twenty-one milking cows; nine heifers; sixteen yearlings, twenty steers, twenty calves, two sheep, twenty-five pigs, one hundred hens and one shorthorn bull."[39]

The Indians had no further interest in the property as far as the government was concerned. "The Indians have no interest in this residential school property. It was sold originally for their benefit and they received the money for it. There is no reversion of title."[40]

That was not the agreement. The Oblates should not have sold the land to the government—it should have gone back to the band. Look at what the Oblates made on that deal. If they bought three hundred acres from the Indians for under $5,000, and then sold two hundred acres back to the government for $70,000, that is a pretty good profit, especially when it was Indian land that the band expected to get back when the church no longer needed it.

The Indians did not get the land back until 1969, more than forty years after the Oblates sold it back to the government. The boarding school closed in the early 1970s. And when we got the land back, we only got part of it. Some did not revert to the reserve. In 1982, the government gave the rest of the land back except the priest house, hall, and rectory, co-op house, and the non-Indian houses. The church hall, rectory, and two houses are still non-reserve.

Not long after the big surrender, the neighbouring Sakimay Reserve was incorporated with the Little Bone Reserve and a meeting was held on Sakimay to admit the Indians of Little Bone. Inspector Graham said the land at Leech Lake would be sold, and after a payment was made to the Little Bone Indians, the balance, after expenses, would belong to the amalgamated Sakimay and Little Bone band.

There's some history there between the Little Bone Reserve at Crescent Lake (also part of Little Bone Reserve) and Cowessess Reserve. Little Bone was thought to be a half-brother of Little Child. They were in the Cypress Hills together, but Little Bone was not a chief there. When the Indians were forced to move east to the Qu'Appelle, some didn't stay in the valley; they moved north around Leech Lake and Crescent Lake. That area was considered Little Bone Reserve and was numbered 73A; Cowessess is number 73.

There were good hay lands there, and lots of times when there was no hay at Crooked Lake there would be hay at Crescent Lake. I have records where Zach, my grandfather, herded all his cows to Crescent Lake to winter there.

There were family connections between Little Bone and Little Child, but because more people from Sakimay went and lived with Little Bone, and Little Bone married a woman from Sakimay, somehow or other those two reserves were amalgamated. My point is that Little Bone's reserve may have started out as a part of Cowessess.

In 1907, Louis O'Soup and a couple of others applied to join the Cowessess Band. O'Soup's application was voted down seventeen to eight. Then the band took a vote to close the reserve to all future applicants; only one person voted to accept future applications.[41]

The following year, Louis O'Soup asked once more to be readmitted to the Cowessess band. Only one of the twenty-nine Indians present voted against him coming back this time.[42]

During the surrender, Alex Gaddie had been the interpreter, and he swung the vote in favour of sale; he expected to get his improvements paid for. He had drained a hay meadow by building a drainage ditch and had hauled rocks off the meadow so that a hay sweep could be used. On Gaddie's behalf, W. C. Thorburn, a lumber, grain, and cattle dealer in Broadview, sent a letter to the Indian commissioner in Winnipeg to acknowledge that the work had been done on that piece of land. Thorburn didn't put a price on Gaddie's improvements but had a few things to say about the surrender process.

> Mr. Gaddie was the one man on the reserve who could have blocked the sale. We were informed at the time the surrender was made that it was Gaddie's vote that decided for surrender. Had he said, no sale,

hardly a man would have voted for it, and I have reason to believe that had Mr. Gaddie not thought that he would be paid for his work on this meadow, he would have refused to part with his share in the land. I talked with Mr. Gaddie several times while the question of surrender was before the Indians and the losing of his hay meadow was the question that Gaddie did not like, and the only reason that he gave for not wishing to sell the land. Afterwards, but before the final meeting when the surrender was made, Gaddie told me that everyone who had made improvements on the land was to be paid for improvements and said, "If the Government will pay me for the work I did on the hay meadow, they can have the land, but I want to be paid for my work if I am not to have the hay."[43]

Thorburn mentioned that Gaddie was the interpreter for the Indians and the men acting for the department when the surrender was made. He wrote, "I am sure he fully understood the question, also that there is enough of the Scotch in his blood to make him fully alive to whether or not his interests are being guarded and that the promise of compensation for improvements on land applied to him personally."[44]

Gaddie was paid thirty-three dollars for his improvements.

It became clear that the Indians didn't own section 8, township 17, range 6, west of the second meridian (which was on the reserve, and had been surrendered). The Hudson's Bay Company owned it. So, the Indians would not get the benefit of the value of that land. The Indians had always believed that piece of land was part of their reserve. The HBC was not using the land and the Indians were allowed to continue to make hay on that section, but they did not receive any other land to make up for it.

Around 1909 or 1910, the Western Canada Colonisation Company purchased a block of the 1907-surrendered Indian land in 17-5 and 17-6 west of the second meridian near Broadview. They resold to Bean of Minneapolis and he resold to individual settlers, who made improvements to their chosen farms. Clients of Hough, Campbell and Ferguson, Barristers and Solicitors from Winnipeg, sold the balance of the property to a number of other purchasers.

Land was not selling well, and some of the farmers who had purchased the land could not make their payments. The land speculator, Mr. Bean, found himself in trouble and unable to pay the department. He was given a couple of breaks and only had to come up with the interest.[45]

In April 1915, the Indians were told they should enclose a pasture area on the reserve to keep their cattle from roaming around during the summer and going off Indian land.

A month later the agent informed the Indians that

> the principal of the school desired to be given permission to build a fence on their reserve, size about one mile by one and a half miles, for the purpose of pasturing during the summer season the cattle belonging to the school. The land which the principal desired to enclose by the fence was of such a measure that it would not by allowing it to be enclosed affect the Indians of the Band in their agricultural or other industries and as the school had no land of its own which could be utilized for a pasture and at the same time have sufficient land for grain growing or other purposes the agent thought that the Indians especially if they took into consideration which they should do the benefits derived from the school would after due consideration give their consent to the proposed fence being built.[46]

In 1911, a delegation of Indians from the reserves in the Treaty 4 area boarded the CPR for Ottawa to discuss the grievances of their bands with officials in the Department of Indian Affairs. The Crooked Lake Agency sent several delegates, including Louis O'Soup (far left) and Alexander Gaddie (far right). Loud Voice from Ochapowace and Kanewinnape from Kahkewistahaw were also part of the delegation. Saskatchewan Archives (RB584)

The school authorities agreed to erect the fence and provide fencing material, including gates, and the Indians could cut the wood. The school would pay one dollar per head annually for all stock over one year old to be pastured inside the fence. The Indians argued the school should pay one dollar for all stock over one year and fifty cents per head for animals under a year. All the Indians at that meeting voted in favour of allowing the school to build the fence for the school pasture.[47]

The superintendent general of Indian Affairs submitted a report to the Privy Council in February 1918. The gist of the report was to consider the possibility of using vacant Indian land in Manitoba, Saskatchewan, and Alberta and to outline how the department could increase production of grain and livestock. It led to the surrender of lands for soldiers returning from the First World War.

> The Minister states that pursuant to the provisions of the several treaties with the Indians, large reserves were set aside out of the public domain, and in order to render the Indians self-sustaining, agents and farmers were appointed to instruct them in agriculture and stock-raising; a system of education in which agriculture formed a chief subject was also established for the youth of the tribes. A considerable degree of success has attended these efforts; rations are no longer issued to able-bodied Indians and they show increasing ability to provide their own maintenance. Last season they harvested 654,644 bushels of grain; their livestock amounts to 22,362 head.
>
> The Minister further states, however, that only a small portion of the land on Indian reserves is under cultivation and that these reserves are for the most part situated in the productive area of the three Provinces and are finely adapted for agriculture and stock-raising.
>
> The Minister has also considered how these idle lands might be brought under cultivation and how the present officers and employees of the Department of Indian Affairs and the Indians themselves might be organized in a scheme to produce supplies of food now so greatly needed. The conclusion has been reached that the appointment of a qualified Commissioner charged with the responsibility of developing such a scheme and carrying it out and clothed with the requisite authority to conduct its activities, would be the first essential to success.[48]

Mr. W. M. Graham, the inspector of Indian Agencies for South Saskatchewan, was appointed commissioner for the Department of Indian Affairs in Manitoba, Saskatchewan, and Alberta and given a list of duties, including:

To make proper arrangements with the Indians for the leasing of reserve lands, which may be needed for grazing, for cultivation or for other purposes, and for the compensation to be paid therefor.

Pursuant to the provision of the War Measures Act, 1914, and of all other authority in that behalf, the sum of $300,000.00 be advanced from the War Appropriation to the Department of Indian Affairs for the purchase of agricultural machinery and implements, seed and live-stock, fence wire and other supplies, and for rentals, salaries, and expenses necessary for the undertaking, the said amount to be refunded to the War Appropriation from revenues arising from sales as they accrue.[49]

This all came together when the Soldier Settlement Board was created after the war to help white soldiers buy or lease farmland when they got back to Canada. The board needed to find land for those returning soldiers and came up with a plan to target Indian land that could be surrendered. They looked straight at the Crooked Lake Agency.

Indian veterans did not get the same support from the government. If there was land available on their reserves, they might get a location ticket, but then that left less land for everyone else and it caused problems on some bands when Indian soldiers came home to their reserves. Besides, it is not the same to use land and occupy it as to own it outright. In the same way that Indians were not allowed to buy a homestead under the *Indian Act*, they were also not given the same benefits as their counterparts under the *Soldier Settlement Act*. The non-Indian soldiers were able to purchase or lease a homestead under the Act, and they could get a loan for livestock or equipment. That was not fair at all. Some of the Indian veterans lived long enough for the government to offer them something, but by then, it was too little and too late.

Application was made in the fall of 1919 to transfer 1,903.56 acres on the Kahkewistahaw Reserve for $28,652.04, and 320 acres on Cowessess Reserve for $3,200.[50]

The land included the east half of section 19, the east half of section 18, the southeast quarter of section 20, and the southwest quarter of section 33, township 17, range 4; the southeast quarter of section 21, the southwest quarter of section 22, the south half of section 3, and the north half of section 5, township 17, range 5, west of the second meridian. These acres were part of the surrender of January 29, 1907.[51]

The recommendation for the transfer to the Soldier Settlement Board was dated in Ottawa, July 24, 1919. It stated:

The land in the Kawkeewistahaw [Kahkewistahaw] reserve was surrendered for sale on the 28th January 1907, and the land in the Cowessess reserve was surrendered on the 29th January, 1907, and the two surrenders were accepted by Orders in Council of the 4th March, 1907.

Section 10 of the Soldier Settlement Act, 1919, provides that "The Board may acquire from His Majesty by purchase upon terms not inconsistent with those of the release or surrender, any Indian lands which, under the Indian Act, have been validly released or surrendered."

Under section 48 of the Indian Act a surrender is required in order to permit the sale, alienation or lease of any portion of an Indian reserve, and under section 49 of the same Act the surrender to be effective, requires to be accepted by His Excellency in Council.

Commissioner Graham and Mr. Walter Govan submitted a report on the 31st May, last, valuing the different sections above referred to, their valuation amounting in the aggregate to $31,852.04 and the valuations were approved by the Minister. The Board has paid 20% of the total valuation.[52]

The land was sold for much less than it was worth. With the transfer, farmers moved in, and the Indians lost out once again.

6
Many Rules

Traditional gatherings, especially sundances, had been outlawed for years. The agent on Ochapowace, around election time in 1911, got word the Indians were thinking about holding a dance because they had heard it was okay to do so again. The agent put a quick stop to that idea. He told the Indians that

> privileges of Chief and Headmen could not be extended to Indians who refuse to conform to the wishes of the Department in matters of progress and education. Progress and education could not be carried on if wasteful practices that have been in disuse here for over 15 years were revived and men who encourage these things were not suitable for Chief and Headmen. A good chief would be one who shows the best example to the Indians by following and attending closely to industrial habits of farming and raising cattle and making a good living for those dependent on him.
>
> It was entirely opposed to the wishes of the Department that Indian's [sic] dances and feasts should be held as it meant a waste of time, substance, injury to their horses and was generally demoralizing. Any person who told them different was not their real friend.[1]

The agent agreed to hold the election but suggested that another one was likely going to be held once he told the department about the sundance.

In order to be a leader, an Indian was supposed to promote earning a living by farming and raising cattle and not behave at all like an Indian. Band members were not to take part in anything that encouraged them to waste time or kept them from their serious work. The government wanted Indians to live like Europeans, always working.

They wanted the Indians to stay on their reserves and not to attend fairs and exhibitions because it might mean they would neglect their farming. The Indian farmers had been winning ribbons at fairs. They were doing a good job with their entries, but suddenly the Indian agent didn't want them to do that any more. If they didn't neglect their farms earlier, what was different? The settlers were at the fairs too. Were they neglecting their farm work?

In a circular, an Indian Affairs official named Duncan Elliot said that a certain amount of recreation should be enjoyed but the behaviour of the Indians should be controlled:

> It is observed with alarm that the holding of dances by the Indians on their reserves is on the increase and that these practices tend to disorganize the efforts which the Department is putting forth to make them self-supporting.
>
> I have, therefore, to direct you to use your utmost endeavours to dissuade the Indians from excessive indulgence in the practice of dancing. You should suppress any dances which cause waste of time, interfere with the occupations of the Indians, unsettle them for serious work, injure their health or encourage them in sloth and idleness. You should also dissuade, and, if possible, prevent them from leaving their reserves for the purpose of attending fairs, exhibitions, etc., when their absence would result in their own farming and other interests being neglected. It is realized that reasonable amusement and recreation should be enjoyed by Indians, but they should not be allowed to dissipate their energies and abandon

Powwow Crooked Lake 1914. Powwow dancing, drumming, and singing were part of sports day activities on reserves. Every dancer had a special outfit; a great hunter, for example, would have a certain kind of beadwork. The government tried to stop traditional gatherings, particularly sundances, to encourage the Indians to forget their ways and focus on farming. Broadview Historical and Museum Association (80:254)

themselves to demoralizing amusements. By the use of tact and firmness, you can obtain control and keep it, and this obstacle to continued progress will then disappear.

The rooms, halls or other places in which Indians congregate should be under constant inspection. They should be scrubbed, fumigated, cleansed or disinfected to prevent the dissemination of disease. The Indians should be instructed in regard to the matter of proper ventilation and the avoidance of over-crowding rooms where public assemblies are being held, and proper arrangement should be made for the shelter of their horses and ponies.[2]

A number of regulations were introduced to keep the Indians in line:

Section 1: It shall be unlawful for any Indian or other person to conduct himself or herself upon this reserve, or any portion thereof in an intemperate or profligate manner and any Indian or other person found so conducting himself or herself shall be deemed an offender against this regulation.

Section 2: It shall be unlawful for any Indian or other person to live on this Indian reserve or any portion of it as man and wife without being legally married. Any Indians or other persons so living together shall be deemed to be offenders against this regulation. Pagan Indians who have been married in accordance with the tribal customs of the band, in which the essence of the marriage is the voluntary union for life of one man and one woman to the exclusion of all others, shall be deemed to be legally married within the meaning of these regulations.

At the time, if you lived common-law, you could not be buried in the Roman Catholic cemetery.

Section 3: It shall be lawful and shall be the duty of the reserve constable or any constable to arrest any offender against the preceding sections and to bring such offender with all convenient dispatch before the Indian Agent, or a Justice of the Peace having jurisdiction and such offender upon conviction shall be liable to a fine of not more than thirty dollars or to imprisonment for not more than thirty days, or both fine and imprisonment at the discretion of such Indian Agent or Justice of the Peace.

Section 4: Excepting members of the band, or the Indian Agent, medical attendant or other employee of the Department of Indian Affairs, or a peace officer, Indian School Teacher, Minister of the Gospel or a Missionary of any religious denomination, no one shall be permitted to be on the reserve without being able to give a satisfactory reason to the Indian Agent or Constables or to the Chief of the Band in the absence of the Indian Agent and the Constable, or to a Councillor of the Band, in the absence of the Indian Agent, the

Marie LeRat, Cowessess Reserve, 1930. Marie Landry was from the Red River area of Manitoba. She married Zachary LeRat, son of Pitawewekijik. They lived in the United States for several years before returning permanently to Cowessess. Saskatchewan Archives (RA24631)

Constable and the Chief, for his or her presence on the reserve and anyone other than these exemptions as above found loitering upon the reserve and failing to give a satisfactory account of himself or herself shall be liable for each offence to a fine not exceeding $5 or to imprisonment for a term not exceeding 10 days.[3]

This regulation was adopted by the Cowessess Band under section 98(c) of the *Indian Act* on June 5, 1925.

7
Priests & Pencils

They put an extension on the boarding school around 1913, using bricks that matched the original ones. At that time, people had to get their bricks from Broadview or Grenfell.

A report on the school from 1913, which was likely written by one of the priests, confirmed that reserve land had been sold for the school. The purchase included eight buildings. The school property extended from Crooked Lake to the Qu'Appelle River, from the hills to the creek, a total of 323 acres including the southeast quarter.

> The present building at present in use are as follows. The priests' house in wood frame, 30 x 20 feet [9 x 6 m], the church is of white wash mortar 62 x 20 feet [19 x 6 m], a house 20 x 20 feet [6 x 6 m] exclusively reserved for the Indians, an ice house of wood frame 12 x 14 feet [3.5 x 4 m], a stable 65 x 20 feet [20 x 6 m] and a general working shop, with the institute proper is a three story building.[1]

The students were given religious instruction in addition to their studies for half a day and then got instruction on gardening and farming and cleaned the stables for the other half day. The older boys learned carpentry and shoemaking.

> The girls go each in turn to the kitchen to learn how to cook. They bake the bread for the children and the staff and can make both boys or girls clothing; they knit the stockings for the school and help to keep house clean [sic]. They also learn laundry work. The older ones go to school half a day and work the other half. The children learn calisthenic drills during one quarter of an hour. Our children have not yet learnt the History of Canada by means of books but by familiar facts which are frequently recalled to their memory. But special care is given to the study of hygiene and they can explain all the maps in their geography from the beginning

to the map of Saskatchewan and a few others. The map of North America is well possessed.

The school has a flag that was very beautiful but by flowing in bad weather it is a little shaggy. We have also a flagpole. Nobody has given us special indication on which day we can follow it, but nevertheless we know it should be on Dominion Day and Victoria Day.

We give our pupils daily three full meals and a small lunch besides the youngest and the weak when any have also a slice of bread in the forenoon.

Dietary Scale:

Bread, 4 loaves at every meal

Sweet tea.

Meat for breakfast about 20 pounds [9 kg]

Potatoes for breakfast about 1 ½ peck [13 L].

Soup (each in turn)

Pea soup, rice soup, potatoes [sic] soup or tomato soup.

Meat for dinner 20 pounds [9 kg]

Potatoes for dinner 1 ½ peck [13 L].

Turnips, carrots etc at dinner

Sauce or gravy at breakfast or dinner.

Fish or baked beans at breakfast or dinner

Fish or porrige [sic] and milk at supper every day.

Dessert for supper every day. Dessert for dinner every day. The desserts consists in pudding, syrup, pies, cooked fruit and occasionally of candies or raw fruit. It is difficult to determine the quantity served to one child even as an average; and I think you can better judge from the following list which will prove that our aim is to vary their food as much as possible. As a whole they eat in a week about.

Flour 3 ½ sacks

Meat 120 lbs [55 kg]

Rice, beans, peas 60 lbs [27 kg],

oatmeal, wheatmeal 25 lbs [11.5 kg],

Sugar. Syrup. molasses 80 lbs [36 kg],

dry fruit 12 lbs [5.5 kg]

butter, lard, grease 30 pounds [13.5 kg]

Potatoes and other vegetables 5 bushels.

The windows are screened and Defiance poison fly is exposed in saucers also a solution of formildehyde [sic].

The very few pupils who have so far shown any tendency to tuberculosis or scrofula[2] have been the object of very special care. eat-

ing at a separate table. where more nutritious food was served and taking as much exercise in the open air as the season could permit. But our aim is to prevent the disease by giving all the pupils blood purifiers and tonic at regular possibility of contagio[n].

The school is drained by means of large tubes made of baked clay which discharge themselves in a running stream a few yards from the main building. We have two baths, two toilet rooms. The pupils bath each week, in summer they go to the lake or the river.

Our water supply is taken from a well in the basement and elevated by a gazoline [sic] engine and a power pump 100 gallons [455 L] capacity per minute in a tank placed in the attic and thence connections distributed all over the house. We have all the water necessary for ordinary purpose but still in order to have an unlimited supply at hand, an other well is dug. The fire protection is abundantly provided for by means of a gazoline [sic] engine and power pump of 100 gallons [455 L] per minute.[3]

The department increased the grant to the Cowessess Boarding

The Marieval Mission School opened in 1898 with six pupils. By 1922, the school grant had increased to accommodate seventy pupils. The Oblates ran the school until 1968, when the Department of Indian Affairs took over. The residential school closed in the 1970s and was torn down in 1999. The Catholic church and rectory on the right were built in the early 1900s. Boarding school students marched to the church for mass every morning. The rectory was home to the priests; the nuns lived at the school. Harold LeRat personal collection

School from support for sixty to seventy students effective April 1, 1923. "The school may therefore recruit up to 70 pupils and in addition, may have in residence, one pupil for each 20 or fraction of that number, or a total of 74 pupils in residence, which should not be exceeded."[4]

On an average attendance of seventy pupils, that grant was just under three thousand dollars. Part of the money was sent directly to the school and the remainder was sent to the Oblate Order: "The Department is paying the grant in the following manner, $120 per capita to you [Reverend J. Carriere, principal of the Cowessess Boarding School], and $45 per capita to the Revs, Pères Oblats."[5]

In 1924, the Department of Education residential school report had some good things to say about the residential school at Marieval.

> My report as to the building, was good. I noted your good class rooms, the hard wood floors, the new single desks, the good black board, the electric light, the satisfactory equipment, save that I

suggested a library. I further noted the cordial relations between the pupils and the teachers. I reported the pupils as obedient and responsive to questioning. I further reported the friendly way in which the pupils played with one another. I had reported at time of the first visit, of the copious supply of garments, bedding, etc., stored ready for use, the cleanliness of the whole school and the evident good health of the children.[6]

The Department of Indian Affairs was really strict about pupil attendance and didn't want students to be at home under the influence of their families. In 1925, pupils at Indian residential schools were allowed up to forty-three days of annual leave in the September quarter, but officials did not think it was a good idea to give the children a Christmas break. The department would not pay grants to the schools if they let the students out without permission. Weekend holidays were not allowed.

> Requests for special or emergency leave for pupils who are urgently needed at home, should be made to the Indian agent who will give approval only when he considers such leave absolutely necessary and after he has the concurrence of the principal, who should understand that grant will be discontinued. Special leave in the case of any pupil should be reported to the Department by the Indian agent. If the medical officer advises that a pupil be sent home for a period because of illness, the Indian agent should be informed, and the principal, when preparing the quarterly return, should not apply for grant for those days the pupil was out of school.
>
> Orphans and children of destitute parents should not be allowed summer holidays, unless satisfactory arrangements can be made for their care when away from school. Principals should not allow annual leave to children who have had to be brought in under escort upon the expiration of former vacations and may refuse holidays to those pupils who truanted during the academic year. Extreme care should be exercised in the case of pupils whose homes are distant from the school. Unless special safeguards concerning their return can be taken, holidays should not be granted.[7]

Some kids didn't get to go home for months if not years at a time. They knew no other life than the residential school.

The priests really tried to get the parents to send their kids to school. One priest wrote in French that loosely translated would go something like this: "The importance of children not to miss school, duty of the parents, very serious. No money could replace the children education. Parents do not keep them back from school for the sake of a few dollars for stooking because those dollars will not get any benefit out of it because God will not bless you."[8]

In 1932 when the inspector visited the residential school at Cowessess, he noted:

> The methods employed by these teachers do not impress me very favourably and they stress the fact that the children do not want to learn. I should say this was cause and effect. The teaching as I saw it today, was merely a question of memorizing and repeating a mass of, to the children, meaningless facts. There was no evidence of anything in the way of motivation or self activity, the key words in education today.
>
> I rather think that special work was prepared for my visit and that the teachers were trying to show me how much the children knew. I advised them that on my next visit the regular routine of the classroom work was to be followed. The children did quite well on the cut and dried work presented but were almost helpless when it came to making any application of same. I feel that regular grading and following a definite Curriculum together with the introduction of more creative work in the classroom would make a very considerable improvement in the work of this school.[9]

There must have been talk of getting rid of the residential school in favour of day school back in the 1930s because in a letter of April 7, 1934, fifty signatures from Cowessess and Sakimay asked to keep the residential school. The petition read: "We the undersigned urge the Department of Indian Affairs to maintain the Indian Residential Schools on our reserves and proclaim entirely opposed to day school."[10] You would think the parents would want to shut down the residential school, but after they went through residential school themselves without any parental support or protection, they lost the ability to parent their own children.

The day school opened for the Indians in 1948. On August 20, 1948, one of the Oblates wrote, "Tomorrow the day school will open. I firmly hope that all the parents are aware of their serious duties to send their children of age to school. Reports have to be made and there is nothing like good reports."[11]

A few months later the community hall was ready. It was a good facility for its time and there was a big celebration. There was even a bowling alley in the basement with two lanes. The hall was used for everything from fowl suppers to wedding dances and Christmas concerts.

One of the priests wrote:

> The official opening of the hall [May 15, 1949] and its blessing was surely a very great success. We should be proud of the friendship given to us, to this Mission, their encouragement for our efforts.

Marieval students beside church, 1900. Students at Marieval received religious and academic instruction for half a day. During the other half day, the boys learned carpentry and farming skills, and the girls learned how to keep a clean house and cook. Saskatchewan Archives (RB10578)

> It is up to us now to keep a good name for our hall, by making it a place of order, of behaviour, of understanding, of friendship, of respect. Please, and please, keep the liquor away from this place, too many to make a few cents come and bootleg. Sooner or later those will be sorry and it will be too late.[12]

The Oblates even bought one of those old, clumsy Bombardier snow machines to get around in the winter. It cost around three thousand dollars, and the Oblates paid for it. We had never seen anything like that before. It was a long time before we started using snowmobiles like there are today.

On September 10, 1951, the day school opened for the Métis. They had to use the old school for a couple of weeks until the new school was ready. The teacher was Mr. St. Onge.[13]

I worked at Marieval as night watchman once in a while during the summer of 1962 and did demolition on the farm buildings I had worked in when I was a boy.

There was a new day school built. The plan was to close the boarding school. By then, many of the kids went to day school, but there were still some boarding at Marieval. In 1962, the school had 139 boarders, 68 boys and 71 girls, and there were 68 day pupils, to total 207.

> According to an Agency member, we would need here room for 40 to 60 pupils per annum for the next 5 years, at least. Our future is very unpredictable. We do not know which way the parents will turn. Actually there is a trend towards coming to our school [as boarders]. From 118 at the beginning of the 1961–62 school year, we came to 137 at the end of the year. This year, we have already in

*Marieval pioneers by church, 1910. The Catholic Church at Marieval
was an important part of the lives of early settlers. The Oblate priests
and sisters of Notre Dame des Missions de Lyon came to the Qu'Appelle
parish at the end of the 1890s to manage the church and residential school.
Saskatchewan Archives (RB10581)*

> school as boarders 139. The parents seem to appreciate more what
> is being done for their children down here. The year 1961–62 saw
> 49 day pupils, while this year 68 turned up. The increase made up
> largely of new comers.[14]

The Oblates ran the boarding school right through until 1968,
when the Department of Indian Affairs took over. In 1975 an addition was built on the day school to add a gym as well as a science lab
and library and an Industrial Arts room. The sisters stayed into the
1970s, when the residential school finally closed. The building was
torn down in 1999.

There were problems in the parish between the Indians, the Métis,
and the settlers. On April 17, 1921, a petition signed by twenty-eight
Indians was presented in favour of creating a separate Indian parish,
with half-breeds included as members.

> Whereas our petition is caused by anti-racial feelings, this griev-
> ance has been submitted for settlement to our past and present
> pastors, by Indians occasionally, but it has availed not a satisfactory
> settlement. Whereas being separate, we have a feeling that we can
> endeavor to exercise our religion with harmony and peaceably.[15]

A postscript added, "Here is a sample of anti racial feeling as expressed
by a Frenchman. 'Next Sunday we will see who owns the pew and I am
going to raise the Devil. This remark was heard by many people.'"[16]

At the end of the same year, the department decided to

> minimize the difficulty that arises in connection with religious belief when recruiting pupils for our Indian Residential schools. No Protestant child shall be assigned to a Roman Catholic school or a school conducted under Roman Catholic auspices, and no Roman Catholic child shall be assigned to a Protestant school or a school conducted under Protestant auspices. In the future, children from Protestant and Roman Catholic homes will be considered eligible for admission respectively to Protestant and Roman Catholic schools only. We rule that wards of the Department of Indian Affairs should be admitted only to institutions conducted under the auspices of the church to which the parents themselves belong. Where there is a dispute, and the agent and the Department cannot decide as to the religious faith of the home, we will then call for a statement from the father of the child, as to his wishes. In the case of an adopted child, the religion of the foster home will be recognized by the Department as that of the child.
>
> When the parents themselves are in disagreement it is clearly established that, except under special circumstances, the father, during his life, has a right to choose in what religion the children are to be brought up, even where the children are illegitimate. The Department reserves the right to make the decision in special cases that are brought to our attention.
>
> I feel this ruling will tend to remove difficulties which arise from various causes, but I do not wish this communication to be the occasion of requests that children be transferred from one school to another, on the grounds of the present decision. We hold that a child that has been resident in a school and may have imbibed religious opinions should remain in that school for the full tuition period.[17]

With all those Catholics in the area, plans got underway to build a new church with a basement. The old log one was torn down.

In order to build a new church it was critical to have charitable donations. The following is a plea for financial support.

> The simple child-like faith of the Indians is the greatest consolation to the missionaries who have them in charge, but descended as they are from a race that lived by the chase and wandered about in search of same, they are slow to acquire the white man's ways of tilling the soil and the results of their more or less indifferent labor are not crowned with any great measure of success. Under the direction of the Black Robe they will perform the work of building a chapel, but to him belongs the task of raising whatever money is required.
>
> Our old chapel, constructed fifty years ago when the Catholic population was still small, has now fallen completely into decay.

Since the chapel was built the Indian Catholic population has more than doubled. A great many half-breeds, living in the surrounding districts, come to worship at our chapel, and in the course of time some six families of white Catholics have been added to their number. If the chapel were in condition it would hold half of our people. We managed with it while it was at all possible, but now the old structure has fallen almost apart.

We need a fairly good sized chapel to accommodate all our people and if it is not built, undoubtedly some of them will drift away. The late lamented Father Carriere, for many years worked hard in an effort to collect the necessary funds for the erection of a new church. Our people corresponded as generously as they could to his noble efforts but you know, Monsignor, better than anybody else, the conditions under which we are working on our Indian Missions.

The Indians are generally very poor; the half-breeds living around them are still poorer, so our chances of collecting money among them are small indeed.[18]

In 1934, there were 5 Polish families, 7 French, 34 Métis, and 104 Indian families at Marieval. There were also 5 French bachelors, 6 Métis bachelors, and 18 male Indians who were not married. In total, 706 parishioners. On Sakimay there were 48 Catholics, on Kahkewistahaw 38, and on Ochapowace 24.[19]

Marieval Residential School staff, 1962; Harold LeRat is standing, back row second from left. Students resided at Marieval even after the day school opened. Harold LeRat personal collection

8
Memories

I was seven when I went to residential school. That was in August or September 1937. I didn't know what school was. I had had no contact with anyone, not even other kids, because my older brother George didn't have kids. He had to raise me after my parents died, and he was only newly married himself. That must have been hard for him. The day he took me to school at Marieval Mission he stopped the team of horses on the east end by the road and said, "See those two doors, that is where you go in." You would think he would have had to sign me in, but the signature on my registration was not my brother's. He was a messy writer and the signature was perfect.

I walked to the doors and I heard a lot of noise on the inside. They were big, heavy doors. I couldn't open them myself. I was just little. One of the boys on the inside must have known I was out there and he opened the door. I walked into that school and I fainted. There were at least fifty boys inside, all yelling. I had never been around that many kids. When I woke up there were all these beds. I didn't know what to do. I just stayed in bed with the covers up.

The other kids seemed to know what to do. They got up and used the bathroom. There was this big sink, like a horse trough. Nobody helped me. When they were all washed, they had to line up. I was supposed to be in the front since I was the smallest, but I didn't know the rules.

George Tanner was the same age as me but he had been there a couple of days and knew what to do. We had to line up for church, then to eat. The girls were on one side and the boys on the other. I didn't know anyone. Boy, it was a rough life to start.

I knew I had to go to school, but my brother hadn't explained any of it to me. I had been alone since I was young, with no other kids around. I didn't know what kids were like, what they did. They made so much noise. I didn't know how to play. I was scared.

The next morning I managed to get to breakfast and then to class. There was only one teacher for the first four grades and only two main classes. I learned fast that I had to listen or I would get punished.

That first day, when I got to the classroom, the teacher didn't recognize me, so I was taken to the principal's office so he could figure out who I was and get me signed in. He didn't know who I was either, and I had to tell him. That was so confusing. One of them must have been the person with the nice handwriting who had signed my papers. That's why it didn't look like my brother's scribbled writing on my school registration form.

By October I had made friends with a few guys, and we knew we didn't like it at school so we decided to run away up the hill and get out of there. At noon the farm boss caught up with us. He said, "Where are you guys going to, Chicago?" He threw us up on his horse and took us back. For our punishment we had to sit in the hallway. Everyone made fun of us.

We didn't give up on escaping. The next year, we ran away again, and that time, they shaved me bald.

One Saturday in January, all of us boys at the school climbed up on the high hill to go sliding. This big, bossy kid told four of us littler kids to get on a toboggan. I was second from the back. You had to hold the guy in front of you and wrap your legs around beside their legs and keep them tucked in tight. We flew down the hill and crashed into someone on an old kind of sleigh with the big iron runners. When we collided, I somehow caught my leg and twisted it backwards and broke it. One of the other guys almost poked out his eye when he hit the iron runner on the other guy's sleigh, and the kid behind me got a bloody nose. We were all hurt.

Nobody offered to take me to a hospital. The nuns looked at my leg and didn't think it was broken. The nurses tried to make me stand up on it. After three weeks, a doctor came from Broadview, and he said I had a broken ankle and put two little splints on it.

I was up in that sick room, called the infirmary, for two months, and they wouldn't let my sister Elsie come up to see me. They sent another girl up. Why couldn't they have sent my sister? I didn't know her that well because she was raised by my older sister Florence, but I was just little and I was always alone.

I could not walk on my ankle and had to be carried down the stairs. Willy Kakakaway from White Bear was one of the older boys. He tried to help by carrying me downstairs. Then he lifted me over the table and set me on the bench on the other side and let me go. I couldn't hold myself up because I could not stand on my ankle, and sure enough, I fell down, right onto the table and into my porridge. I still had to eat that porridge. I finally got out of the infirmary after weeks stuck up there, and I landed in my porridge!

I limped for a whole year after I broke that ankle.

I don't remember any of the kind of food they talked about feeding the kids at the school in the earlier years. We got porridge for breakfast, but that was it, no meat, ever, for breakfast. And the porridge was lumpy, salty, and hard. We had to eat it all up too. They never threw anything away. That's why we ended up with sour potatoes. They cooked them in a big pot and by the time we got to the bottom of it, the potatoes had turned sour. We used to carry big hankies to the table and try to wrap those potatoes up and get them outside to throw them away, and not get caught. You had to clean up everything on your plate.

I was amazed to hear that anyone got sweet tea. I don't remember that. Turnips and parsnips, we got those. And every Friday we had fish. At least we didn't get porridge for supper. We always had something to eat.

When my dad went to school he was not allowed to speak Saulteaux or Cree. The kids would get beaten if they did, so when his older kids went to school, dad said not to speak Cree or you will get beat up. The older ones all spoke the Indian languages at home, but because Elsie and I were in school after our parents died, we lost our language. I learned a few words when relatives came to visit, but back then kids had to be quiet when you had company so I would go out of the room, and because I stayed away, I didn't learn.

We got to go home from school for Christmas and Easter and for Sunday a couple of times a year. My brother George drove down to the mission on Sunday to see me as often as he could, but he lived on the south end of the reserve and that was about six miles away. Many of the parents came on Sundays in June when they weren't working. They would pitch tents. I didn't get visitors like that. My parents were gone and George was always working.

My sister Elsie was in the same school but in the girls' wing, and then Dick, my youngest brother, came when he was old enough, but we were not allowed to talk to each other.

The first summer I went home to my brother's farm I was eight. George asked me if I had learned how to cut hay in school and I said no. So he said, "Well, you'll learn," and I started by raking hay that year.

The priests and nuns were mean to some kids who got in trouble, so I learned to be a good boy. I started to work in the barns. I was good with animals, so I spent all my time in the barns. Sometimes I would play hooky and stay out there, so I didn't get much education. My cousin Ernest Lerat used to work with the animals too, and he kind of looked after me. He was thirteen or fourteen, but I was just cheeky enough to know I didn't want to be in school. I wanted to go out in the barns, even on Saturday, but Ernest said no, I couldn't go out there because the bigger boys always had a gang fight in the pump house while the farm instructor was away. There were two gangs. They threw cans and stuff.

Willy Kakakaway, the guy who carried me downstairs when I broke my ankle, was always my guardian. He was a good man. And I had Ernest looking out for me. Willy left school when I was ten or eleven but by then, I could kind of look out for myself. I was always a loner, still am. I just stayed to myself and then I would not get into trouble. I had one friend who I won't name, well we were friends until he got into the vanilla extract and got drunk, and then I had to stay clear of that or I would have been in trouble.

When I was about ten, the school had a big 1030 McCormick-Deering tractor with no power steering. I was so little I had to stand up on the clutch to push it in, and I had trouble turning the steering wheel. It was so stiff. The first time I had to drive that thing, pulling the plough, doing summer fallow, everything went okay until I got to the end of the field and had to turn. I knocked trees down and fences. I learned that I needed lots of time to stop the tractor and that I needed to start turning earlier when I was getting to the end of the field.

The farm instructor must have put in a word for me because I didn't go to class much.

Ernest and I had twenty-one head of cows to milk. Ernest did eleven and I did ten. We got up so early that we were almost done milking by the time the instructor got out to the barn. That milking had a good side because once we were done, we had to do the separating (to get the cream from the milk). We had the cream and the milk right there, all we needed was some fruit and a pound of butter and bread and we could go out and eat in the bush. We snitched from the kitchen, until we got caught one day. I was on lookout and this big nun came in and caught Ernest. She slapped him on the face and then the priest called us up to his room and gave us a good talking to. We had to promise not to do that again or we would not be able to keep milking.

Ernest woke me up early every morning. We didn't have any watches, and this one day I was pretty sure it was too early, but we snuck downstairs. Sure enough, it was just after midnight, and so we had to sneak back up the stairs and go back to bed.

Another night, when I was about twelve, we were going to sneak out and go to a fiddle dance. Three of us planned to go down the fire escape. We had to go by the nuns' bedroom window on the first landing. Two of us slid down easy, nice and quiet. The third guy thumped down, landed a little hard, and made too much noise. We saw the nuns' light come on and knew we were caught, so we ran around to the back door and up the stairs. The boy's keeper was waiting for us. We were darned lucky we didn't get punished.

I guess we didn't learn too fast that running away didn't work. The third time, I ran off with two other guys from the Kahkewistahaw reserve. Wouldn't you know, we met cousin Ernest's mom on the hill on a little bush road. We couldn't avoid her. There was no way to hide or to go around her. She knew we were running away, and she picked up a big stick and told us to go back.

Instead, we went over to my sister's place along the lake. She thought we were on a school outing. We had been there before, when we had skating parties. So she gave us some lunch and put some buns in a bag, and we left.

We walked from four in the afternoon until almost midnight. It was snowing in the afternoon and we were walking in about a foot of snow. We were about four miles from the mission, up on the hill, on a sleigh road that was used to get to the mission. Every time we heard someone coming, we'd run and hide. We were soaked to the skin and cold.

They were out looking for us with the station wagon the school had bought. We saw the lights coming, and they sure enough had us. They picked us up and took us around to tell our families we were okay. It was the middle of the night by then. My brother George said, "So, why were you running away. Did you want money?" and I said yes, and he gave me fifty cents.

By the time we got back to the school at 2:30 a.m. or so, the priest was waiting. We were already cold but he made us put our feet in cold water and shower in cold water and then we went to the priest's room and there was the boys' keeper. He was a big guy. We knew we were going to get it. He had a wide strap. The biggest guy started crying before he even got the strap. The priest held me down. I got the strap bare-assed. I could not sit down proper for weeks. That was the last time I ran away.

We could only go to residential school until grade eight. I didn't get my full grade because I worked half days at the school farm. I really maybe got grade two or three. I knew how to multiply but not divide. I learned what I know now by reading. I guess I'm what you call self-taught. I always read a lot. I picked up every western book I could get my hands on, and eventually I could read a pocketbook in a night. In school, I just worked in the barn and went to class until I could get out of there.

There was no high school around so most Indian students didn't go on from grade school. W. J. D. Kerley, the Indian agent, asked me when I got out that summer if I would like to go to school at Notre Dame College at Wilcox, Saskatchewan. I knew I didn't have the proper qualifications, the proper education, but he said I would be able to catch up. I wanted to go, but it was up to my brother, and he didn't get around to signing the papers. I found out years later when I was talking to some of the older men that my brother George thought I would be better off working for him.

George paid me two dollars a week every Saturday so I could go to town. Plus, I got extra money when I needed it to buy clothes or other things. It was decent pay for me at fourteen. After I got my pay on Saturday, I'd ride to Broadview, which is about ten miles, with fifteen or twenty other guys so we could fight. We had little gangs of fighters and we fought each other or the white boys. Sometimes we won.

I was a pretty good pool player, so sometimes I would gamble with my two dollars and shoot pool. I could make good money at the pool table.

When it was ploughing time, I had to go out in the morning, walk to where the horses were, and chase them home so we could hitch them up to the plough. Instead of walking back to the farm, I'd just jump on the back of the saddle horse that was at the end of the line behind the others, and with no bridle I'd ride along and my mount would herd the others home.

We had to drive the horses about four miles to get to the breaking where we had to plough, then take them back home again at night to put them in the pasture. George drove six horses in front and I had four behind.

Once the horses got a good furrow going, they would just follow along, but at the end of a furrow, you had to lift the ploughshares out of the ground to turn. Then when you got going straight down the field again, you would sink the plough back in. I could turn okay, but I was not strong enough to sink the ploughshares back into the ground. Once we did the turn, George would hang his lines. The horses would just keep on going in the furrow, and he would run back to me and sink the plough, then hurry back to his horses.

If I was going along and hit a stone, I would fly up into the air.

I enjoyed when I was able to start doing the full farm and field work, but there was always that darned ploughing every spring. By the time I finished the field, the grass was up again on the first part.

One day we had to come home early when a big, black cloud came up and the thunder and lightening was something fierce. The horses were spooked. The only way I could stop them was when George told me to run them into the bush.

I wanted to be a jockey, but there was no such thing as training to be a jockey when I was a kid. I just started riding at seven or eight, and I got to be good at it. Leigh Brennan, a horse buyer and supplier who ran a livery barn in Broadview, used to come to the horse races on the reserve and knew I could ride. When I was about nine he talked to my brother and asked him if I could ride for him, and George said no. Of course, I didn't know about that conversation until much later. When I was eleven, Brennan came to talk right to me, and I started to work as a jockey for him. I was a natural rider. Every town had horse races, and this guy had two thoroughbreds. One of my other brothers, Clifford, and a guy named George Kay, who was a professional jockey, would help me to get to the races and to learn. George Kay was from Sakimay but he rode in Regina and used to come home to run in the bush races. They looked after me and told me when I was doing anything wrong. So I guess that was training, but not from a jockey school or anything. I rode every day, and I was a pretty good jockey until I grew too much to meet the weight requirements.

My love of horses goes way back as far as I can remember. At about five or six I took an old feed pail over to a foal and realized that when she put her head down I could hang over her neck. She got used to me doing that and finally I got up enough nerve to throw my leg over her and get on her back. She bucked. Off I went.

We didn't have saddle horses to begin with, just workhorses, so they were big. That is how I got to Broadview on a Saturday for the fights. I might have been nine, and I'd meet those other guys, riding on one of those big old workhorses. We'd go to town; beat each other up, and then we'd all ride home together. That was a lot of fun.

At fourteen I started breaking horses for Brennan so he could sell them broke. That was 1944. I got ten dollars a head and could make forty dollars a month in a busy season. I could break four horses a month. The men working as hired hands on farms only got about thirty by comparison. I did that breaking work until I was about twenty.

Some years were really tough on the reserve. The report of the superintendent of Indian Agencies shows how bad things were in 1941.

> Cowessess Reserve is really desperate. At the meeting with this Band they informed me that they only received $1.00 a cord for wood sold in the Valley, and the market is very poor. They sell to a store at the Crooked Lake School and to another store off the Reserve, north of the river. This is a desperate situation for the poor Indians to have to take $1.00 a cord after chopping the wood and hauling it maybe several miles. However, I am in hopes of probably getting a better market for the wood at Melville, where we may be able to trade some of it off in exchange for flour. We might also be able to sell it for cash and realize a better price for it than the Indians are getting locally. I instructed the Agent to go to Melville this week and see what he can do in the way of finding a market. The heavy snow may have some effect on the sales but we have to do all we can to explore the situation and find a better market if possible. However, the Cowessess Indians will have to be assisted, there is no question of this, and I shall take up later by special letter.
>
> It is deplorable to think that the Indians of the Cowessess Reserve were at one time fairly prosperous Indians. They had quite a few more cattle; they did considerable more farming and are fairly intelligent Indians, more on the half-breed type. This year they only seeded 92 acres of wheat and a little over 400 acres of oats, simply because they had no land fit to seed. It was noticed in travelling around that most of the land that has gone back, which is several thousand acres, we at one time had a greater production farm on this reserve, consisting of 3,000 acres. This land was turned over to the Indians and then went back to weeds, as well as several hundred acres which the Indians farmed themselves. The worst of it is that most of the land is now twitch grass.

Men of Cowessess around 1920. Left to right, standing: J. N. LeRat, F. J. Delorme; seated: Ted Delorme, Paul Peltier. Harold LeRat personal collection

> Cowessess, as I have said before, is a real worry as the Indians are not only very hard up but also disgruntled. The Band will have to have some flour, feed grain and also seed.[1]

In the late 1940s, the Indians started farming again and operated a band farm called the Leafy Spurge. They picked the name because they were trying to control the leafy spurge weed problem. That weed still causes us trouble today.

We always lived off the land, picked wild turnips and rhubarb, so when the Indians had to start farming their ten- or twenty-acre plots in the Cypress Hills, they caught on and did as well as the settlers. But to provide a hoe and a pick and expect the Indians to work only with hand tools, like they did after treaty, well that wasn't really farming, it was just expanded gardening.

Even when they moved to Crooked Lake, the older Indians showed they were good farmers, and then their children were forced to go to boarding schools and everything changed. By the time the kids left school, the older farmers were ready for them to take over, but they couldn't even get a loan at the bank because they were Indians.

Band money was used to give horses to some of the Indians coming out of school, and when you get something for nothing you don't always appreciate it. Up to that time, everyone farmed. Many people lost interest after welfare came in. Sometimes, I think that the government wanted to control us, and maybe they didn't want us to be successful. Maybe the settlers were jealous of our success. So some Indians gave up. Others didn't. In the 1930s, there were a number of successful farmers on the Cowessess reserve, and they did well, but after welfare, we lost self-pride. If people depend on government for money and if you think the government will always be there to hand out the money, then at some point you just say, "Well, they took our land away and so they have to feed us." That's what happened, and it was a big mistake.

When I was a teenager, I had a trap line, and every day I'd take about an eight-mile trip from slough to slough setting muskrat traps. If I left around noon, I'd get back by midnight. Rats travel in their dens at night, so I could get lots of them if I checked all the traps. I had about fifty stops along my route.

My brother Gordon—we called him Dick—was about four years younger than me, and he lived with my sister Florence. He would come with me on horseback to trap muskrats. The first time I took him along it was spring. There was still snow around, and the ice on the slough had a couple of feet of water on it. I wanted Dick to know how to set the traps properly, so we rode out onto the ice to a couple of muskrat houses and I set the traps. Dick just watched. He was learning. On the third slough, Dick's horse was getting nervous and would not stand and wait for us. It kept throwing its head up and down. Dick had to bend down to set the traps and the horse was right behind him. The second time the horse put its head down, it slipped, and the shoulder of the horse hit Dick in the ass. He went headfirst into the icy water. It was a cold day and he was soaking wet.

Dick got up and looked that horse in the eye and swore. I told him to get straight home and dry out and then I headed on to the next slough. When I looked back, there he was, sitting on the hill wringing out his socks. I thought he would go back and get warmed up. He was only maybe twelve or thirteen, just a kid. I went to look at the next den. The rats were inside so I started to set the traps. Then I heard horses hooves galloping. There came Dick, whipping that horse on both sides.

There was a little creek running into the slough I was in, and like I said there was still ice under the water. I looked at Dick barrelling toward me, and I thought, "He's going to tumble if he keeps doing what he's doing." Sure enough. The horse made a summersault, and off he went.

Dick's saddle pad was made of a coyote hide. Mine was made of a badger hide. We just tied the hide on with a rope that went around the horse's belly. When Dick flew off, the saddle pad rode up over the horse's head and covered her eyes. The horse got up and just stood there; she couldn't see and couldn't move.

Dick got up too, walked back to his horse, swore again, and took off the horse's blindfold. I of course told him he should have gone home, but he just rode off into heavy bush. I went after him, and we made a bonfire. Dick undressed to his shorts and hung his clothes on the willows to dry.

That is only one of the funny stories about my brother Dick. We had some good times.

Depending on the price of furs and before welfare came in, a lot of Indians trapped to make money in the winter. In the 1940s they put a quota on muskrat and I could only trap thirty animals, so all my brothers and uncles got quota and I filled them all up. At that time, you got 75 cents to a dollar and sometimes as much as $2.50 for a muskrat. The best weasel could bring $8, and for mink I got from $40 to $150. By the mid 1970s, long-haired furs were up around $150 to $200 for coyote and $75 to $175 for fox, so I hunted and trapped.

That winter, a buddy of mine and I made $8,000 on pelts. We had six working greyhounds that year. Prices dropped after that and people stopped wearing fur, so I quit trapping.

My ancestors wandered back and forth between Canada and the United States, but Cowessess was the home they came back to. My grandfather Zach was with his father, Pitawewekijik, in Little Child's band at time of treaty. Zach met Marie Landry after he went to the United States. She was from the Red River area in Manitoba. They got married and lived as Americans from about 1887 to 1880, when they came back to live permanently on Cowessess.

The American government issued a quarter of land to each male Indian as their allotment. Pitawewekijik and Zach LeRat would each have had 160 acres. When Zach died in 1930, two quarters went to my grandmother. That would have been Zach's quarter and the land he inherited from his father, Pitawewekijik. Marie Landry, my grandmother, died on Cowessess in 1948.

Zach had a treaty card from the United States. Zach's children, including my father, Solomon, may have had dual citizenship.

Back then, like I said, you had to get a permit from the Indian agent to sell anything. Most of the Indians didn't take cash. They bartered. They were good traders in those days. The Indians were honest. They would go into the bush and cut a load of wood, then go and almost beg for a bloody permit, and then the next day drive it to town to sell the wood for $1.50 a load.

Not only that, but Indian Affairs wanted the Indians to pay dues for cutting fence posts or firewood. All that work of cutting and hauling wood for almost nothing, and then we were expected to pay dues to boot.

W. J. D. Kerley, the agent, sent a resolution from the Cowessess band about the dues:

> This Band is very much opposed to paying any dues and this is the general feeling throughout the Agency. In my own opinion I think it would be better if dues were charged on green wood, pickets and logs and dry wood be exempt, since I think that we should encourage the Indians to cut dry wood to relieve the local fuel shortage and because dry wood is a fire hazard on the reserve.[2]

The response was that

> standing timber on an Indian Reserve belongs to the full Band

membership and as one of the capital assets of the whole Band no individual has a right to take it without compensating the Band for its interest in it. To illustrate: when an Indian makes cordwood or cuts fence pickets for sale the raw material does not belong to him but to the Band of which he is a member and the royalty he is asked to pay is only the value of the standing trees. For example, if a man cuts and sells cordwood at $5.00 a cord he pays twenty or thirty cents a cord for the raw material and the other $4.70 or $4.80 which he receives is in payment of his labour in preparing it for the market.

There seems to be a general impression abroad that the imposition of timber dues on an Indian who cuts wood products from his own Reserve is in the nature of a tax imposed by the Government for its own purposes. This of course is not so as every cent collected is credited to the capital funds of the Band who own the raw material from which the manufactured product is made. To do otherwise would be penalizing those who do not cut and sell timber produce as timber assets would be used up without any compensation to them for its loss.[3]

My brothers were still getting permits when they hauled grain in 1948 when I took my first load of wheat in to the elevator in Broad-

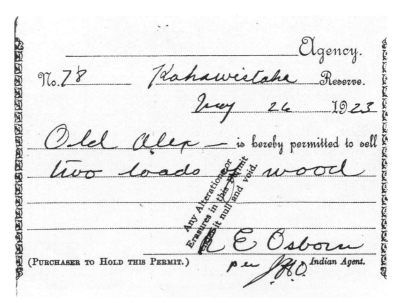

Before Indians could sell wood, grain, cattle, or other farm products they had to get a permit from the Indian agent. He also decided if they would be allowed to purchase supplies off the reserve, including groceries. Courtesy Broadview Historical and Museum Association.

view. I didn't get a permit. The elevator agent was writing out a cash ticket for me, and before he finished he kind of hesitated and then wrote a little bit more and then looked again, and he said, "Where's your permit?" I said, "I don't have any; those are my horses and my sleigh and that is my wheat and I don't need a permit." He never said another word, just stared for a minute and started writing again. I could have got into trouble because I didn't use a permit, but I never did.

I never did brand my cattle with the Indian Affairs brand either. The government brand was "ID" for Indian Department.

The band bought cattle and lent them out to individual Indian farmers. The deal they made was that if you got five cows for five years then you gave the band five heifers and the cows were yours. They had a revolving fund, which was a good deal, but I wanted to have my own cattle, not Indian Affairs animals.

Even though you had to get a permit to sell government cattle, it didn't make them hard to sell. We had a band pasture where everyone would put their cattle. We would round them all up in the fall and the buyers would come out from Grenfell and Broadview.

All the band cattle had the ID brand on the right hip and then each Indian had his own brand, say on the left shoulder. When you got the five cows from the band, you put on the ID brand, then when the cows had calves, you would still put the ID brand on the calves, in addition to your own brand.

That is why I would never use the Indian Affairs brand, because some people had forty or fifty cows and calves and they all had ID brands and maybe only ten belonged to Indian Affairs. If the cattle were sold and the owner didn't have his own brand on with the ID brand, all the money went to Indian Affairs. The Indian who owned the cattle would have to prove he had paid back the debt before the department would give him a cheque for his cattle.

My brother George helped me start farming because I had worked for him for so many years. He just gave me his equipment so I could break up land.

I bought my own cattle. I didn't want to take a cent from Indian Affairs. I got my own brand made. In the 1950s, I paid three hundred dollars for one cow because I wanted the best milkers around.

I had horses of my own by then, and I got my first contract working for the oil company after they bought the right to drill on Cowessess. They dug two wells, found a little oil, but capped them. They had to dig pits for the waste oil and water, and those had to be filled in. So

Making hay was a daily routine every July unless it rained or there was a sports day. Left to right: Gordon (Dick) Lerat, Buddy Lerat, and Harold LeRat. The child (standing) is Harold's niece Linda. Harold LeRat personal collection

that is what I did. I used my team of horses and scrapers like they used then to build roads, and I covered the holes.

Band members got a decent amount of money when they paid for the drilling rights, and I used most of mine to buy that three-hun-dred-dollar cow.

In the 1940s, Kerley, the agent, started buying tractors for the In-dian farmers. George had to sell all his horses. We had worked with horses up until that time. I was so mad about him selling the horses that I went off to work for a couple of years, left the farm.

When tractors came in, a lot more Indians quit farming because if the tractor ran out of gas or quit on them, they couldn't fix it and had to get the Indian agent. They didn't understand motors and tractors. The younger Indians learned about cars and motors, but farming went downhill after the 1940s.

Some bands bought fuel for their farmers and some of them didn't have to pay it back. I didn't agree with that because that money they were using to help only one farmer was supposed to be used for ev-eryone else on the reserve.

At one time we used the buffalo for everything, and all parts of the animal were used. When they were gone, there was no way to make

*Powwow on Cowessess
in 1940s. Harold LeRat
personal collection*

our living. Then there was welfare, and look how there got to be so
much waste. Everything changed. It was too easy to get a big welfare
cheque. But I was stubborn. I was poor, very poor. But I would not
accept welfare.

In the late 1940s, it changed from the ration system, where my
grandmother and the old people and destitutes got rations. That
didn't mean they got money, just food to get by. Rations ended when
the welfare system came in when Diefenbaker was the prime minister.
I was eighteen when the farm instructor started handing out welfare
money. I knew what welfare was. They put it on the radio for months.
I argued with that farm instructor about it. I knew welfare was going
to spoil us. Even the able-bodied quit working. If you worked you
could not get welfare. Some men never worked again.

I worked in summer and went trapping in winter. Sometimes I got
pogey (unemployment insurance from working), but I didn't want to
take welfare.

Now there are five generations that have known nothing but welfare. Many don't even hunt any more because there is money to buy
meat at the store. With a large family, it seemed you could not work

hard enough to earn as much as welfare paid. That is pretty sad. It means the system didn't work.

Treaty payment day still happens every spring on the reserve, and we still get $5 like when the treaties were signed. They used to hand out ammunition to each family, but that has died off a bit. I think the elders still get a few .22 shells when the officials come to make the payments. Until a person turns eighteen, parents pick up the payment for their kids. Usually the RCMP are there and Indian Affairs, same as in the 1800s. I agree with my nephew, Gordon Lerat, Dick's son. He says they haven't calculated any inflation into that five bucks we receive. Most people think Indians get big money on Treaty Day. That is pretty funny.

What Gordon remembers most about Treaty Day when he was a kid in the late 1950s and into the 1960s is that parents had to take their kids through the x-ray machine to check for TB when they went to get their payment. That's because there was still tuberculosis around then, and if you had it, you were sent to the sanatorium in Fort Qu'Appelle and they kept you there until you were better. That was pretty scary for a kid if they found anything on the x-ray because they knew they would have to go away from their families.

I never was too interested in going to Treaty Day. If I go next year, I'll get a whole $20 because I haven't picked up my payment for three years now.

Sports days and powwows were held together in the summer. Years back, there would be fiddle dancing, games, road races, foot races for everybody. The Indians used to run a lot.

There was powwow dancing and people sang. The government tried to stop the regular powwows and fiddle dances. They didn't want us to do any of the traditional Indian things, especially sundances, and we would get in trouble if the dances were held.

There were horse races at those sports days. People would come from Broadview, and Indian horsemen came from the Fort Qu'Appelle area, as far away as White Bear, by Carlyle, and from the Kamsack reserves. We would all compete. There were trotter races. Some guys brought their professional horses out from Regina, thoroughbreds too. There was a track on each reserve. We didn't have the money to go elsewhere, so we had to have something to do at home.

In the 1950s we stopped having horse races, and eventually even

Indian Pony Race, Broadview. After towns started springing up on the prairie, sports days became the major event of the summer. The Cowessess Reserve bush races drew competitors from reserves around Broadview, Fort Qu'Appelle, Carlyle, and Kamsack. Several generations of Indian horsemen made names for themselves on the rodeo circuit and racetracks of Canada and the United States. Saskatchewan Archives (RA253-8)

the sports days ended, the tracks grew over, and then it was just maybe a ball tournament and that was it.

We got the right to vote in 1960. I was glad. We had to go to Broadview to vote, but by the second election, I realized they were making the Indians vote separately. We were in a different line. I guess that was because we lived on the reserve and were in a particular polling station, because it is still like that. I still vote, but I didn't like the way voting was done because it was easy to tell how the Indians voted because they report the results by polling station.

I was able to get into my first beer parlour, the Ehrle Hotel in Regina, when I was only sixteen. My friend said to just mess up my hair and they would let me in. We used to go up on the north side of the valley to drink. The bar owners would let us into the hotels in Grayson, Dubuc, and Killaly because they didn't know us up there. It seems like those bartenders knew when the cops were coming and they'd tell us to get out the back way.

On the Thursday or Friday night before we were going to be allowed to drink in the bars, I was with some of my buddies in Broadview. We stayed until closing time and promised to be back first thing at eleven in the morning when they opened because we could drink legally then. The thing was that shortly after lunch, I realized it wasn't fun anymore. There was no challenge, no risk once it was okay to be in there, so I went home.

If Christopher Columbus had not been lost we might never have been called Indians. Right from the time of contact with the Europeans, we were called Indians, because those explorers thought they had reached the East when they had only got to North America. Anyway, we were called Indians for a couple of hundred years, but that changed recently. Indian is not considered a proper term anymore. Our people are called First Nations people now. That is why the reserves are no longer known as reserves. Cowessess is now the Cowessess First Nation.

It took a long time, but on December 7, 1995, the Cowessess First Nation successfully ratified its Treaty Land Entitlement Agreement. The reserve received $46,662,314 to make up for lands they should have had dating back more than 120 years, since treaty in 1874. The settlement was supposed to make up for the acres that didn't get properly allocated at the time of treaty. Some of the band members were out hunting, travelling, or visiting and did not get counted, and there was all the confusion of O'Soup and Little Child being split between the Cypress Hills and Crooked Lake.

When the payment was calculated, the federal government contributed 70 percent and the province of Saskatchewan 30 percent. The monetary settlement was to be paid out over the next twelve years. Under the agreement, the reserve had to buy a minimum of 53,312 acres of land which had to revert to reserve status.[4]

In 1997, the issue of land that was illegally surrendered to the federal government in 1907 went to the Court of Queen's Bench in Regina. The lawsuit claimed that 20,704 acres of the band's land was illegally surrendered and later sold to third parties. Negotiations continue.

The Cowessess First Nation has around three thousand members. About five hundred live on reserve. Cowessess is located about 160 kilometres east of Regina, approximately 20 kilometres north of Broadview, and consists of 12,000 hectares of land.

Golfers come for miles to the Last Oak Golf and Country Club, our eighteen-hole course. There are teepee camps that recognize the culture and history of our people, and we have a mall complete with gas and grocery, post office, bank, laundry, and other businesses.

9
Little Child's Legacy

It has been almost a decade since I started to think about writing this book about my reserve, and in those years many things have changed; others, for good or bad, stay the same. That is life, and it will go on long after I've finished telling my story.

In 1874, the world changed for Chief Little Child and for my ancestors in the Cypress Hills. Treaty came, and their freedom to roam the prairies ended. They were forced to leave those hills behind and build a new future at Crooked Lake.

There are those of us who choose to stay on Cowessess Reserve No. 73. My children, grandchildren, and great-grandchildren and those that come after will find a place to live their lives. Some will stay here and others will travel to interesting cities and countries, free to roam once again, but in a much different world.

No matter where the Cowessess people go or what they do, the thing that holds us all together is our past. Little Child's legacy is here on this land, in our hearts and our memory.

Sorting It Out

Pronunciation of names as well as their written form had many variations. Indians had names that sounded very similar, which also confused Indian Affairs officials and proved to be a challenge when tracing family histories.

There was no written language and nothing to simplify the spelling of the complicated and often lengthy collection of vowels and consonants that made up the Indians' names.

Indian Affairs officials and the clergy basically guessed at the spelling. Many different variations can be found for any given name. Consider the name O'Soup, which means backfat. In research documents the name has many variations, including Ousupe and Osoup.

Cowessess, being of mixed blood, had different names in Cree and in Saulteaux. He was known as Kawezauce (quee-wee-sonce, Little Child) in Saulteaux, and Kawassis (kaw-wah-sis, Little Boy) in Cree. He is also recorded as Couwecess, Cowess, and Cowesses.

Pitawewekijik, which in Cree means Sounding through the Sky, is pronounced peh-tah-way-way-key-zick; in Chippewa, which is Saulteaux, it is Pitowewekiizhik (pee-tah-way-way-key-stick).

LeRat, which is French for the rat, sounds like lee-raw. LeRat was the original spelling; more recent generations use Lerat.

Nepapheness, Night Bird, is pronounced knee-paw-pan-ace. His name is spelled several ways in written records, including Neepappeeness, Nepahpeniss, Neeahpenace, and Nepapeiness.

Aisaican, clarified sugar, sounds like nah-say-i-gun.

Kanaswaywetung, Two Voice, is pronounced can-ass-way-wee-tung. The name is spelled in many ways and sometimes it is hard to tell that the names refer to the same individual. Other spellings include Kanaswaymetung and Kanaswaywetang.

Notes

LAC/PAC: Library and Archives Canada   PAM: Public Archives of Manitoba
SAB: Saskatchewan Archives Board.

Ancestors

[1] There are conflicting theories about Pitawewekijik and whether he was indeed the man who was known as Pierre LeRat or if he was instead Pierre's brother Pieskana-hapit, who was called Francis. Francis was part of the band in 1879. It is possible that our family history search has confused the two men. For the purposes of this book, we have assumed that Pitawewekijik was the man who swam the river, got the name Pierre LeRat, became part of Little Child's band, lived part of his life in the United States, and was Harold LeRat's great-grandfather who died on the Cowessess Reserve in 1911.

Chapter 1 — An "X" Changes Everything

[1] Treaty No. 4 between Her Majesty the Queen and the Cree and Saulteaux Tribes of Indians at Qu'Appelle and Fort Ellice (Ottawa: Queen's Printer, 1966), p. 6.

[2] Ibid., p. 4.

[3] Memorandum signed by W. J. Christie, 28 October 1874, PAC, RG 10 Black 4063.

[4] Articles of Treaty concluded 15 Sept. 1874, copy 135, signed between the Cree, Saulteaux, and other Indians and the Lieutenant Governor of Manitoba and the North-West Territories, Honourable Alexander Morris, Minister of the Interior David Laird, and William Joseph Christie, Esq., of Brockville, Ont.

[5] A. Morris, *The Treaties of Canada with the Indians of Manitoba and the North-West Territories* (Toronto: Coles Publishing Co., 1971), pp. 330–31.

[6] Summary of Documentation, Cowessess Band, Document Number 118, 1874.

[7] Trevor Harriot, *River in a Dry Land: A Prairie Passage* (Toronto: Stoddard, 2000), p. 9.

[8] Memorandum, W. J. Christie, 28 Oct. 1874.

[9] W. J. Christie to the Minister of the Interior, October 1875, Lieutenant-Governor's Collection, PAM, MG12 B1-1102.

[10] Ibid.

[11] Chiefs at Cypress Hills to Alexander Morris, Governor of Manitoba, 20 April 1876, Lieutenant Governor's Collection, PAM, 1247.

Chapter 2 — Leaving Those Hills Behind

[1] Sergeant Z. M. Hamilton to Mr. W. M. Graham, Indian Commissioner, Regina, 3 March 1932, Glenbow, M8097, Graham, box 1, file 1.

[2] J. M. Walsh, Inspector commanding Fort Walsh, to Lieutenant Colonel A. G. Irvine, Assistant Commissioner, NWMP, Fort Macleod, 27 May 1877, Appendix F, Mounted Police Report; see also ibid.

[3] Ibid.

[4] Sergeant Z. M. Hamilton to Mr. W. M. Graham, Indian Commissioner, Regina, 3 March 1932, Glenbow, M8097, Graham, box 1 file 1.

[5] Dominion of Canada, Annual Report, Dept. of Indian Affairs, 1881, p. 131.

[6] Report, Deputy Superintendent General Indian Affairs, 1879, p. 95, on-line, LAC <http://www.collectionscanada.ca/indianaffairs/020010-119.02-e.php?uid=1437&uidc=ID &queryString=>.

[7] Ibid., p. 96.

[8] "Links with the Past," Crooked Lake Agency, NWT, Broadview Museum, no. 225.

[9] Information on location of Maple Creek home farm provided by Clay Yarshenko, Maple Creek, 22 Oct. 1999.

[10] Edgar Dewdney to Superintendent General of Indian Affairs, 13 Nov. 1880, PAC, RG 10, vol. 3716, file 24, 800.

[11] Dominion of Canada, Sessional Papers, vol. 5, Fourth Session of the Fourth Parliament, 1882, SAB 6–8, vol. xv, no. 5, p. xxxi.

[12] Ibid.

[13] Dominion of Canada, Annual Report, Dept. of Indian Affairs, 1881, p. 38.

[14] Notice of meeting between Dewdney and Sioux, Cree, and Assiniboine Chiefs at Qu'Appelle, 1881, Indian Affairs, PAC, RG 10, vol. 3768, file 33642.

[15] Ibid.

[16] Ibid. Scab was known to be a mange in sheep.

[17] Ibid.

[18] Ibid.

[19] Ibid.

[20] Dominion of Canada, Annual Report, Dept. of Indian Affairs, 1881, p. 37.

[21] Ibid., p. 56.

[22] Ibid., pp. 45–49.

[23] Ibid., pp. 54–57.

[24] Report of the Commissioner, North-West Mounted Police, 1880, p. 13.

[25] Dominion of Canada, Annual Report, Dept. of Indian Affairs, 1881, p. 54.

[26] Ibid.

[27] Ibid.

[28] Report of the Commissioner, North-West Mounted Police, 1881, Report of Surgeon Robert Miller, p. 30.

[29] Dominion of Canada, Sessional Papers, Fourth Session of the Fourth Parliament, 1882, vol. 5, SAB 6–8, vol. xv, no. 5, p. xxxii.

[30] Report of the Commissioner, North-West Mounted Police, 1881, Report of Surgeon Robert Miller, p. 30.

[31] Ibid., p. 29.

[32] Ibid., p. 30.

[33] Dominion of Canada, Annual Report, Dept. of Indian Affairs, 1882, pp. 205–6.

[34] Indian Agent McDonald, June 1882, Document 2459, LeRat/Ungar research files.

[35] *Settlers and Rebels: Being the Official Reports to Parliament of the Activities of the Royal North-West Mounted Police, 1882–1885* (Toronto: Coles Publishing, 1973) p. 3.

[36] Indian Commissioner to Superintendent General, Winnipeg, 12 Sept. 1882, PAC, Indian Affairs, 9441.

37 Annual Report, Dept. of Indian Affairs, 1883, p. 73, on-line, LAC, <http://www.collectionscanada.ca/indianaffairs/020010-111.01-e.php?gbr%5B0%5D%5BcolNme%5D=Year&gbr%5B1%5D%5BcolNme%5D=DOCUMENT_ID&gbrf=TRUE&gbr%5B0%5D%5Bstart%5D=1883&gbr%5B0%5D%5Border%5D=ASC&gbr%5B0%5D%5Bend%5D=1883>.

38 Ibid., p. 74.

39 Ibid, p. 73.

40 Indian Commissioner E. Dewdney to Superintendent General of Indian Affairs, 14 April 1883, 6330, LeRat/Ungar research files.

41 Office of the Commissioner of Indian Affairs, Winnipeg, to the Superintendent General of Indian Affairs, Ottawa, 25 May 1883, PAC, Indian Affairs, RG 10.

42 Annual Report, Dept. of Indian Affairs, 1883, p. 71.

43 Kenneth J. Tyler, "Interim Report, A History of the Cowessess Band, 1874–1911" (unpublished paper prepared for the Federation of Saskatchewan Indians, 1975), p. 22.

44 Indian Agent McDonald to E. Galt, Esq., 12 July 1882, no. 476, PARC, file 673/30-2-73.

45 One chain equals 66 feet; 80 chains equal one mile; 10 square chains equal one acre, on-line <http://www.treefarmer.com/land_ownership_and_measurement.htm>.

46 Treaty No. 4 document, Indian Reserve No. 73, SAB, R834-32PQ.

47 Annual Report, Dept. of Indian Affairs, 1883, p. 71.

48 Ibid., p. 75.

49 Ibid., p. 71.

50 Ibid., p. 104.

51 John Peter Turner, *The North-West Mounted Police, 1873–1893*, vol. 2 (Ottawa: King's Printer, 1950), p. 8.

52 Annual Report, Dept. of Indian Affairs, 1883, p. 98.

53 Ibid., p. 99.

Chapter 3 — Resistance

1 Report from Surveyor Allan Patrick 17728, Indian Affairs RG, vol. 3853, file 78, 418.

2 Louis Osoup to anonymous female friend, 10 Sept. 1884, Riel Documents, LAC, RG 13, Justice, series F-2, vol. 805, reel C-1228, p. 530.

3 Letter from Louis O'Soup, Lac Croche, 10 Sept. 1884, translation of RG 13, reel C-1228, document number 34, p. 530; translation PAM, MG3D1 no. 623, p. 8.

4 G. P. Campbell, *Diary of 1885: The Country as Seen by G. P. Campbell,* Broadview Museum.

5 "Links with the Past," Number 225, Crooked Lake Agency, NWT, Broadview Museum.

6 Blair Stonechild and Bill Waiser, *Loyal till Death: Indians and the North-West Rebellion* (Calgary: Fifth House, 1997), p. 84.

7 Notice dated 6 May 1885, Regina, signed by E. Dewdney, Indian Commissioner, LeRat/Ungar research files.

8 G. P. Campbell, *Diary of 1885.*

9 Marie Adeline Jordens, "Memoirs, Rainville History," pp. 34–35, Broadview Museum.

10 G. P. Campbell, *Diary of 1885.*

11 Llweyn Friars (née Sefton), "Descendents of Thomas Wilson" (2000, family history provided by Bert Sefton, gleaned from Mattie Sefton (née Wilson), "Broadview Centennial Tribute," 1982), p. 5.

12 Blair Stonechild and Bill Waiser, *Loyal till Death,* p. 255.

[13] Annie I. Yule, *Grit and Growth: The Story of Grenfell* (Grenfell Historical Committee, 1980).

[14] Mavis Anderson and Orville Fitzgerald, eds., *The Good Old Days of Broadview* (Broadview, Sask.: 1955).

[15] "Bringing Home the Bacon," Oblate Archives, Ottawa, L 1021.M27R 57.

[16] Dominion of Canada, *Sessional Papers*, 1889, no. 16, p. 168.

[17] Deputy Minister of the Interior to L. Vankoughnet, Deputy Superintendent General of Indian Affairs, Ottawa, 4 March 1886, no. 106817, file 104900-27230, LeRat/Ungar research files.

[18] Minutes, Crooked Lake Agency, 27 July 1888, SAB, R-E 3692.

[19] Office of Indian Affairs, Regina, to Superintendent General Indian Affairs, Ottawa, 30 April 1886, LAC, RG 10, Indian Affairs, vol. 3911, reel C-10160, file 111404.

[20] Frank W. Anderson, *Outlaws of Saskatchewan, True Tales of Crime and Criminals from Our Storied Past* (Humboldt, Sask.: Gopher Books, 1999), pp. 5–9.

[21] Marie Adeline Jordens, "Memoirs, Rainville History," pp. 52–53.

[22] *Daily Sun*, 12 Oct. 1887, "With the Press Party: An Indian Farm—Western Agricultural Exhibition—Tenderfoot Journalists in the Great Lone Land. Special Correspondence to the Sun. Broadview, N.W.T., 1 Oct.," PAM, no. 10, MG1B29.

[23] Ibid.

[24] Ibid.

[25] *Daily Sun*, 15 Oct. 1887, "With the Press Party," PAM, no. 13, MG1B29.

[26] *Daily Sun*, 19 Oct. 1887, "With the Press Party," PAM, no. 16, MG1B29.

[27] *Daily Sun*, 15 Oct. 1887, "With the Press Party," PAM, no. 13, MG1B29.

[28] *Daily Sun*, 19 Oct. 1887, "With the Press Party," PAM, no. 17, MG1B29.

[29] *Daily Sun*, 5 Nov. 1887, "With the Press Party," PAM, no. 29, MG1B29.

[30] Ibid.

[31] Marie Adeline Jordens, "Memoirs, Rainville History," pp. 56–58.

[32] Llweyn Friars, "Descendents of Thomas Wilson," pp. 3–4.

[33] Marie Adeline Jordens, "Memoirs, Rainville History," p. 68.

Chapter 4 — Warrior Farmers

[1] District of Assiniboia, NWT, *Sessional Papers*, A 1892, no. 14, Crooked Lake Agency, 12 Aug. 1891, pp. 39–41.

[2] Minutes, Crooked Lake Agency, 3 Feb. 1891, SAB, R-E 3692.

[3] Minutes, Crooked Lake Agency, 7 Oct. 1891, SAB, R-E 3692.

[4] District of Assiniboia, NWT, *Sessional Papers*, A 1892, no. 14, Crooked Lake Agency, 12 Aug. 1891, pp. 39–41.

[5] Ibid.

[6] Ibid.

[7] Ibid.

[8] Ibid.

[9] Ibid.

[10] Ibid.

[11] Minutes, Crooked Lake Agency, 15 April 1892, SAB, R-E 3692.

[12] Dominion of Canada, *Sessional Papers*, 1897, no. 14, Annual Report, Dept. of Indian Affairs, 1896, p. 228.

[13] Secretary to Deputy Superintendent General of Indian Affairs, 21 October 1893, RG10, vol. 8052, file 673/31-2-3-73.

[14] Assistant Secretary McNeill to Right of Way Agent, CPR West Thomas Nixon, Esq., Winnipeg, 15 October 1897, RG10, vol. 8052, file 673/31-2-3-73.

[15] Minutes, Crooked Lake Agency, 9 April 1894, SAB, R-E 3692.

[16] Indian Agent McDonald to Indian Commissioner, Regina, 9 June 1894, RG 10, vol. 3911, file 11, reel C-10160.

[17] Minutes, Crooked Lake Agency, 25 Sept. 1894, SAB, R-E 3692.

[18] Minutes, Crooked Lake Agency, 5 Nov. 1894, SAB, R-E 3692.

[19] Dominion of Canada, *Sessional Papers,* 1896, no. 14, Annual Report, Dept. of Indian Affairs, 1895, p. 95.

[20] Ibid., p. 96.

[21] Ibid.

[22] Dominion of Canada, *Sessional Papers,* 1897, no. 14, Annual Report, Dept. of Indian Affairs, 1896, p. 229.

[23] Minutes, Crooked Lake Agency, 11 Feb. 1895, SAB, R-E 3692.

[24] Dominion of Canada, *Sessional Papers,* 1896, no. 14, Annual Report, Dept. of Indian Affairs, 1895, p. 97.

[25] Horses bred and raised by the Indians; mustangs.

[26] A contagious respiratory disease, like pneumonia, that can be transmitted to humans.

[27] Dominion of Canada, *Sessional Papers,* 1896, no. 14, Annual Report, Dept. of Indian Affairs, 1895, p. 96.

[28] Ibid., p. 98.

[29] Dominion of Canada, *Sessional Papers,* 1897, no. 14, Annual Report, Dept. of Indian Affairs, 1896, p. 228.

[30] Dominion of Canada, *Sessional Papers,* 1896, no. 14, Annual Report, Dept. of Indian Affairs, 1895, p. 99.

[31] Minutes and Petition, Crooked Lake Agency, 25 Feb. 1896.

[32] Dominion of Canada, *Sessional Papers,* 1896, no. 14, Annual Report, Dept. of Indian Affairs, 1895, p. 100.

[33] Ibid.

[34] Dominion of Canada, *Sessional Papers,* 1897, no. 14, Annual Report, Dept. of Indian Affairs, 1896, p. 224.

[35] Ibid., p. 226.

[36] Ibid., p. 225.

[37] Ibid.

[38] Ibid., p. 226.

[39] Ibid., p. 225.

[40] Ibid.

[41] Ibid., p. 226.

[42] Ibid.

[43] Ibid., p. 224.

[44] Ibid., p. 226.

[45] Ibid., p. 224.

[46] Ibid., p. 225.

[47] Ibid., p. 226.

[48] Ibid., p. 225.

[49] Ibid., p. 224.

[50] Ibid.

[51] Ibid., p. 225.

[52] Ibid., p. 224.

[53] Ibid., p. 225.

[54] Ibid., p. 227.

[55] Ibid., pp. 225–26.

[56] Ibid., p. 224.

[57] Ibid., p. 227.

[58] Ibid., p. 225.

[59] *Sessional Papers,* vol. 35, no. 11, 1900, SAB, p. 323.

[60] Ibid., p. 141.

[61] Minutes, Crooked Lake Agency, 28 June 1898, SAB, R-E 3692.

[62] Minutes, Crooked Lake Agency, 6 July 1898, SAB, R-E 3692.

[63] Not purebred or registered.

[64] *Sessional Papers,* vol. 35, no. 11, 1900, SAB, p. 141.

[65] Ibid.

[66] Minutes, Cowessess Band, 18 Sept. 1899, SAB, R-E 3692.

[67] *Sessional Papers,* vol. 35, no. 11, 1900, SAB, p. 142.

Chapter 5 — Stolen Land, Broken Promises

[1] Minutes, Cowessess Band, 4 and 9 July 1900, SAB, R-E 3692.

[2] Ibid.

[3] Ibid.

[4] Report, Crooked Lake Agency, North-West Territories, Qu'Appelle Inspectorate, Fort Qu'Appelle, 16 Sept. 1901.

[5] Indian Agent Magnus Begg to Secretary, Dept. of Indian Affairs, Ottawa, 19 Aug. 1901, Indian Affairs RG10, vol. 3996, file 206, 070-8.

[6] Assistant Secretary to Magnus Begg, Indian Agent, 29 August 1901, Indian Affairs RG10, vol. 3996, file 206, 070-8.

[7] Minutes, Cowessess Band Meeting, 9 April 1900, SAB, R-E 3692.

[8] Ibid.

[9] Secretary to Magnus Begg, Indian Agent, 7 November 1902, Indian Affairs RG 10, vol. 3996, file 206, 070-8.

[10] Magnus Begg, Indian Agent, to Indian Affairs, 5 August 1903, Indian Affairs RG 10, vol. 3996, file 206, 070-8.

[11] David Laird, Indian Commissioner, to Dept. of Indian Affairs, 23 August 1902, Indian Affairs RG 10, vol. 3996, file 206, 070-8.

[12] Ibid.

[13] Ibid.

[14] Petition to Honourable Minister of the Interior, PAC, RG 10, vol. 3732, file 26623.

[15] Indian Agent, Broadview, to David Laird, Commissioner of Indian Affairs, 1 June 1904, PAC, RG 10, v.ol. 3561, file 82/4.

[16] J. A. Sutherland to J. A. McKenna, Assistant Indian Commissioner, Winnipeg, 14 June 1904, PAC, RG 10, vol. 3561, file 82/4.

[17] J. A. McKenna, Assistant Indian Commissioner, to Acting Indian Agent, Crooked Lake Agency, 20 June 1904, PAC, RG10, vol. 3561, file 82/4.

[18] Memorandum, Ottawa, 3 July 1906, PAC, RG 10, vol. 3732, file 26623.

[19] Minutes, Crooked Lake Agency, 6 June 1906, SAB, R-E 3692.

[20] Ibid.

[21] William Graham, Balcarres, Sask., to Mr. Oliver, 19 June 1906, 294189, PAC, RG 10, vol. 3732, file 26623.

[22] Ibid.

[23] Minutes, Crooked Lake Agency, Reserve No. 73, 21 Jan. 1907, SAB, R-E 3692.

[24] Minutes, Crooked Lake Agency, Reserve No. 73, 29 Jan. 1907, SAB, R-E 3692.

[25] Dominion of Canada, Province of Saskatchewan, form no. 66, signed 2 Feb. 1907, LeRat/Ungar research files.

[26] Minutes, Crooked Lake Agency, Reserve No. 73, 29 Jan. 1907, SAB, R-E 3692.

[27] Dominion of Canada, Province of Saskatchewan, form no. 66, signed 2 Feb. 1907.

[28] Memorandum signed by Wilfrid Laurier, approved 4 Mar. 1907, o/c, RG 2/1, PC 409.

[29] Minutes, Reserve Number 71, 22 Jan. 1907, SAB, R-E 3692.

[30] Minutes, Reserve Number 72, 23 Jan. 1907, SAB, R-E 3692.

[31] Minutes, Reserve Number 72, 28 Jan. 1907, SAB, R-E 3692.

[32] Minutes, Reserve Number 71, 9 Feb. 1907, SAB, R-E 3692.

[33] Memorandum for Deputy Minister, 20 Oct. 1909, LAC, RG 10, Indian Affairs, vol. 3732, reel C-10128, file 26623.

[34] Minutes, Crooked Lake Agency, 28 May 1907, SAB, R-E 3692.

[35] Ibid.

[36] Memo, Dept. of Citizenship and Immigration to Superintendent, Crooked Lake Agency, 7 Dec. 1959, file 011176, SAB, R-E 3692.

[37] Chief, Reserves and Trusts Division, Dept. of Citizenship and Immigration, to Superintendent, Crooked Lake Agency, regarding Cowessess Residential School land, 5 Feb. 1960, file 001523, SAB, R-E 3692.

[38] Memo, Dept. of Citizenship and Immigration to Superintendent, Crooked Lake Agency, 7 Dec. 1959, file 011176, SAB, R-E 3692.

[39] Levi Thomson, Thomson, Kennedy and Lord, Barristers, Solicitors, Notaries, Wolseley, Sask., 2 Oct. 1925, Oblate Archives, L1027.M27L, 113.

[40] Memo, Dept. of Citizenship and Immigration to Superintendent, Crooked Lake Agency, 7 Dec. 1959, file 011176, SAB, R-E 3692.

[41] Minutes, Crooked Lake Agency, 14 Mar. 1907, SAB, R-E 3692.

[42] Minutes, Crooked Lake Agency, 18 July 1908, SAB, R-E 3692.

[43] W. C. Thorburn, Broadview, Sask., to David Laird, Indian Commissioner, Winnipeg (copy), 24 June 1908, LAC, RG 10, vol. 3732, reel C-10128, file 26623.

[44] Ibid.

[45] Solicitors Blake, Lash, Anglin and Cassels, Toronto, to Secretary, Dept. of Indian Affairs, Ottawa, 15 Nov. 1915, 484997, Cowessess First Nation files.

[46] Meeting, Cowessess Band, 12 May 1915, SAB, R-E 3692.

[47] Ibid.

[48] Certified copy of a Report of the Committee of the Privy Council, approved by His Excellency, the Governor General, 16 Feb. 1918, Privy Council of Canada, PC 393, signed by Rodolphe Boudreau, Clerk of the Privy Council, LeRat/Ungar research files.

[49] Ibid.

[50] Certified extract from the minutes of a meeting of the Treasury Board, 27 Aug. 1919, approved by His Excellency the Governor General in Canada, 30 Aug. 1919, 526914, LeRat/Ungar research files.

[51] Ibid.

[52] Recommendation, Dept. of Indian Affairs, Ottawa, 24 July 1919, PAC, Indian Affairs RG10, vol. 7534, file 26, 108-2 (401108-2).

Chapter 6 — Many Rules

[1] Minutes, Ochapowace Reserve, 13 June 1911, SAB, R-E 3692.

[2] Circular from Duncan Elliot to Thomas Graham, Ottawa, 15 Dec. 1921, LeRat/Ungar research files.

[3] Minutes, Crooked Lake, 5 June 1925, SAB, R-E 3692.

Chapter 7 — Priests & Pencils

[1] Response to circular of 5 Dec. 1912, sent from Cowessess Boarding School, Marieval,

Crooked Lake, 5 Jan. 1913, to J. D. McLean, Secretary of Indian Affairs, Ottawa, Oblate Archives, L1021.M27R 56.

[2] Tuberculosis of the lymph nodes of the neck.

[3] Response to circular of 5 Dec. 1912, sent from Cowessess Boarding School, Marieval, Crooked Lake, 5 Jan. 1913, to J. D. McLean, Secretary of Indian Affairs, Ottawa, Oblate Archives, L1021.M27R 56.

[4] Letter from E. Taylor, Indian Agent, Crooked Lakes, Broadview, 9 March 1922, Oblate Archives, Marieval, L 1027.M27L 68.

[5] Russel T. Ferrier, Superintendent of Indian Education, to Reverend J. Carriere, OMI, Principal, Cowessess Boarding School, Marieval, Sask., April 1922, Oblate Archives, L 1027.M27L 69.

[6] James Little, School Inspector, Wolseley, Sask., to Reverend Carriere, Marieval, Sask., 15 Jan. 1924, Oblate Archives, Ottawa. Les Archives, Scholasticat Du Sacre-Coeur

[7] Russel T. Ferrier, Superintendent of Indian Education, Ottawa, to Church Authorities, Principals and Department Representatives, 20 May 1925, Oblate Archives, L1027.M27L 109.

[8] Manitoba Box, Oblate Archives, Ottawa, Ontario, L1021.M27C.

[9] Excepts from Provincial School Inspector Winters's Report, 9 Sept. 1932, signed by Lucien Ouellette.

[10] Oblate Archives, Ottawa, L102.M27L 185.

[11] Manitoba Box, Oblate Archives, Ottawa, L1021.M27C.

[12] Ibid.

[13] Ibid.

[14] Recording by P. G. Gelinas, Cowessess Indian Residential School, Marieval (via Grayson) Sask., Archives Deschatelets, L1021.M27R.

[15] Petition, Trustee for the Church, signed by Chief or Indians, to His Grace Archbishop Mathieu, Regina, Sask., 17 April 1921, Oblate Archives, L1021.M27L 64.

[16] Ibid.

[17] Duncan C. Scott, Deputy Superintendent General, Dept. of Indian Affairs, Ottawa, to Reverend Father Guy, OMI, University of Ottawa, 24 Dec. 1921, Oblate Archives, L1021.M27L 79.

[18] "In the Mission Field," Les Archives Scolasticat Du Sacre-Coeur, Lebret, Sask., Oblate Archives, L1021.M27R 20.

[19] Manitoba Box, Oblate Archives, L1021.M27C.

Chapter 8 — Memories

[1] M. Christianson, General Superintendent of Indian Agencies, Report on the Crooked Lake Agency, 26 Nov. 1941, LAC, RG 10, vol. 8052, file 673/20-7-2-73.

[2] W. J. D. Kerley, Indian Agent, Crooked Lake Agency, Broadview, Sask., 6 Jan. 1944, PAC, Indian Affairs RG 10, vol. 8052, file 673/20-7-2-73.

[3] Director to W. J. D. Kerley, Indian Agent, Broadview, Sask., 18 Jan. 1944, PAC, Indian Affairs, RG 10, vol. 8052, file 673/20-7-2-73.

[4] Government of Saskatchewan, news release, 14 Mar. 1996, on-line <http://www.sasknet.sk.ca/saskgov/newsrel/1996Mar/096.096.96031406.html>.

Index

trapping 60, 70, 135–136, 141
Treaty 2 77, 87
Treaty 4 14, 15, 18, 19, 27, 29, 36, 108,
 147, 149
Treaty 6 39
Treaty Day 142
Treaty Land Entitlement Agreement
 144
treaty negotiations 14, 16, 22, 34, 35
treaty number 16
treaty promises 13, 15, 17, 33, 34, 35,
 36, 86, 97, 98, 104, 109, 142
treaty restrictions 37
treaty rights 90
Troy, Sask. 49
tuberculosis 117, 142
Turtle Mountain, North Dakota 8, 9,
 11, 49, 56, 90
United States 14, 19, 20, 27, 32, 36, 39,
 55, 56, 90, 93, 115, 137, 143, 147
veterans 110

Wahpekaneraup 81
Walsh, James Morrow 19, 23, 26, 32,
 148
Wapamouse 81
War Measures Act 110
Wawasecapp 17
Weed Creek 45, 87, 104
welfare 4, 135, 136, 141
White, Roger 92
Whitewood 6, 43, 74, 96
White Bear First Nation 128, 142
Wilson, Elizabeth 67
Wilson, Thomas 53, 67
Winnipeg 15, 18, 43, 49, 62, 94, 96,
 97, 106, 107
Wolseley 43, 62, 153
women 57–58, 91
 and residential schools 77, 81
Wright, Mr. 91, 93
Yellow Calf 4, 45, 53, 55, 87
Yellow Quill 34, 35

About the Writer

Linda Ungar farmed for twenty years on the north side of the Qu'Appelle Valley near the small community of Dubuc, Saskatchewan, not far from the Cowessess First Nation. To supplement the farm income, she worked in radio and television as a copywriter and later wrote columns and articles on agriculture and Aboriginal issues. She took an active role in preservation of rural services and the farm women's movement.

Linda has worked in government communications, advertising, and eventually came to specialize in access to information and privacy legislation. She now lives in Yellowknife, Northwest Territories, but returns often to visit family and friends in Saskatchewan and spend time at the cottage at Crooked Lake.